THE JEWISH WORLD
FAMILY HAGGADAH

THE JEWISH WORLD FAMILY HAGGADAH

ZION OZERI
PHOTOGRAPHY

SHOSHANA SILBERMAN
EDITOR

ibooks
new york

DISTRIBUTED BY PUBLISHERS GROUP WEST

A PUBLICATION OF IBOOKS, INC.

COPYRIGHT © 2006 IBOOKS

PHOTOGRAPHS COPYRIGHT © 2004 BY ZION OZERI
PHOTOGRAPHS PRINTED BY DAVID WONG, NEW YORK, NEW YORK

COVER ART COPYRIGHT © 2004 BY ZION OZERI

IBOOKS, INC.
24 WEST 25TH STREET
NEW YORK, NY 10010

ISBN 1-59687-315-9
SECOND IBOOKS, INC. PRINTING FEBRUARY 2006
10 9 8 7 6 5 4 3 2

PRINTED IN CANADA

About The Editor

Dr. Shoshana Silberman is an author whose books include *A Family Haggadah* I & II, *The Whole Megillah (Almost)*, *Tiku Shofar: A High Holiday Mahzor*, *Siddur Shema Yisrael: A Shabbat Family Prayerbook* and *Family Rhymes for Jewish Times*. Dr. Silberman has been a teacher and principal who has led workshops across North America. She is currently a consultant for the Auerbach Central Agency for Jewish Education.

Shoshana Silberman holds a B.S. from Columbia University, a B.H.L. from Gratz College, a M.S.T. from The University of Chicago, and an Ed.D. from Temple University.

About The Photographer

Zion Ozeri is a world-renowned photographer, exploring the jewish experience. His work explores a personal search for connection in a world impacted by exile and loss. Born in Israel to immigrants from Yemen, he grew up among people whose lives had been shaken by displacement. In his photographs, Ozeri encounters Jewish communities scattered across the world, and in them he finds a sense of home, of familiar customs and shared experiences. His images speak to all who have altered, shaped and reinvented their traditions, fusing old and new, familiar and unfamiliar, creating rich, modern and meaningful ways of life.

Infused with a cross-cultural perspective and a mission to explore the diversity of Jewish life around the world, he captures the differences between these communities, as well as the many profound similarities that have endured across time and place. His photographs consider the forces that have kept Jews together as a people throughout the millennia, and reflect on what binds Jews to their faith and to one another. Ultimately, his work asks viewers to ponder universal questions about what unites people in their common humanity.

Zion Ozeri graduated from the Fashion Institute of Technology and Pratt Institute, both in New York City, where he received a Bachelor of Fine Arts degree. He published several books and many photographic essays in magazines & newspapers. His photographs had been exhibited in many museums and galleries worldwide. (**www.ZionOzeri.com, www.TheJewishLens.com**)

Dedication

Byron Preiss
1953-2005

This Haggadah is dedicated to Byron Preiss, who conceived and believed in this book with his heart and soul. He understood the importance of its eternal message of hope, faith and freedom.

We are forever grateful.

This Haggadah—a telling—combining words and images, emanates from a sense of profound love and values, instilled in me by my parents, Hayim and Nadra (Grafi) Ozeri. It is dedicated with deep love and gratitude to my wife, Ellen de Jonge Ozeri. May my children, Gilad, Ayala Alexandra, and my stepchildren Gabrielle and Chloe be inspired to carry on.

Zion Ozeri, November 2004

This Haggadah is in memory of my dear parents, Samuel Riber and Betty Ribner Borok (z"l). It honors my "treasures" … my children Shmuel, Lisa, and Gabriel, and son and daughter-in-law, Daniel and Sara, as well as my grandchildren Noam, Jonah, Yaakov, Adira, Meir and Chana. May they carry on the family tradition of lively and engaging sedarim, where all is discussed respectfully "in the name of heaven" and sung with enthusiasm and joy. It also honors my husband Mel, my true love, my friend and partner, who has been a source of inspiration to me and my family.

Shoshana Silberman, November 2004

The Secret, Mevaseret Zion Absorption Center, Israel, 1990

Introduction

The importance of the Haggadah—the retelling of the Israelites' exodus from Egypt as traditionally recited over the past millenia—is not only in celebrating liberty and a birth of a nation, but also in the values embedded within it. The old generations' principles relating to identity and community are still with us today, impressing our eyes and touching our hearts. I hope that my work sheds light on the Haggadah's narrative and helps connect past and present.

—Zion Ozeri

"Ma Nishtana…?" Why is this Haggadah different? Why is it special?

First and foremost, *The Jewish World Family Haggadah* features the captivating photographs of Zion Ozeri. As we recite the words of the Haggadah and elaborate on the meaning of the Exodus, viewing these beautiful photographs connects us to Jews around the world. We are not alone as we ask questions and debate interpretations of text. People in many countries, with diverse cultures, are all telling the Passover story, as if they themselves left Egypt.

Second, this Haggadah also connects us to generations past who all felt the sacred obligation to relate the story to the next generation. This Haggdah not only tells the story, but also features commentaries old and new, Ashkenazic and Sephardic, traditional and liberal, male and female, original and learned. It celebrates the wisdom of "Clal Yisrael" – all Israel.

Finally, the Haggadah text has been supplemented not only with commentaries but also discussion questions, activities and songs to make the seder interactive and engaging to teenagers and adults. Also included are many ideas to have the seder come alive for children. Thus, *The Jewish World Family Haggadah* is geared to the multigenerational participants seated at most seder tables. Family and friends of all ages will feel welcome to participate.

This Passover, through the photographs, commentaries, discussions and activities, bring the past and present together and invite the Jews around the world to join you!

—Shoshana Silberman

How Best To Use This Haggadah

If you are serving as leader or co-leaders of your seder, it is vital to read the Haggadah before the seder to become familiar with the text. Next, think about ideas and themes that seem especially appealing to you. It is also helpful to consider the needs of the participants who will be present, especially if they differ in age and background. Then select commentaries, discussion questions and activities that you think will be stimulating and a good match (or balance) for attendees. Also select photographs on which you would like to focus. Leave time to explore an issue fully, rather than rushing to complete every item. Leave something for next year! Even if you have a definite plan, however, leave room for spontaneity.

Plan ahead! There are a number of things to prepare in advance. A list of the required and optional items you will need for your seder preparation follows directly. Having them ready will make your seder run smoothly and increase interest and participation.

Jewish Day School, Harare, Zimbabwe, 1998

Setting the Seder Table

Holiday candles

Wine or grape juice
(enough for four cups per person)

Wine cups for each person

Matzah

Seder plate

Cup for Elijah filled with wine

Three matzot
(covered)

Afikomen bag or special napkin

Pillows for reclining

Salt water or lemon juice for dipping

Cup, bowl, and towel for washing

Haggadah for each person

The Seder Plate

Beitzah	roasted egg	בֵּיצָה
Karpas	parsley, celery, or potato	כַּרְפַּס
Z'roa	roasted bone (beet or avocado seed for vegetarians)	זְרוֹעַ
Charoset	Ashkenazim use chopped apples & nuts, wine & honey, flavored with cinnamon. Sephardim use chopped figs, dates, raisins, apricots or oranges, and other spices. Some Israelis add a banana.	חֲרֹסֶת
Maror	bitter herb (usually horseradish)	מָרוֹר
Chazeret	usually romaine lettuce (for the Hillel sandwich)	חֲזֶרֶת

Optional Seder Items

(Below are other items you might use or prepare for your seder. More details about them are provided throughout this Haggadah.)

Cup for Miriam filled with water

Extra matzah for the Matzah of Hope

Flowers for the table

Individual seder plates
(Staple 3 cupcake papers together. One is for the egg and parsley, the second is for charoset, the third is for salt water.)[1]

Olives as a symbol of peace
(The olive branch is a universal symbol of peace, associated with the dove in the story of Noah and the ark. Olives can be served after the hard-boiled eggs, prior to the meal.)

An orange as a symbol of inclusion

Scallions to use during Dayenu

Hard-boiled eggs for all participants
(served prior to the meal)

Afikomen gifts

Seder Trivia Game

Duplicated Passover story, cut in sections

Cups numbered 1, 2, 3, and 4 to indicate which cup of wine is being blessed

Pictures of frogs, stuffed animals or plastic frogs

Echad Mi Yodea "certificates"
(for knowing all the answers)

Puppets or pictures for Had Gadya

Omer Calendar
(for counting the days of the Omer)

Omer Tzedakah Box
(for giving tzedakah during the time of the Omer)

A "kittel" (a white robe), worn traditionally by the seder leader

Wearing a kittel has various interpretations: the color white signifies freedom; the robe reminds us of the Temple service offered at Passover by the priests who wore special robes. The kittel reminds us of the sacredness of life and the need to act quickly to work for freedom.

Lighting the Festival Candles

Kindling Holiday Lights, Mumbai, (Bombay), India, 2001

It has been said: "An angel is not fit to stand in the shoes of the eve-of-Pesach Jew." With the extensive preparations behind, we are now ready to light the festival lights.[2]

Before sunset, we light the festival candles and recite this blessing:
(*On Shabbat, we add the words in brackets*)

בָּרוּךְ אַתָּה יי אֱלֹהֵינוּ מֶלֶךְ הָעוֹלָם אֲשֶׁר קִדְּשָׁנוּ בְּמִצְוֹתָיו וְצִוָּנוּ לְהַדְלִיק נֵר שֶׁל
(שַׁבָּת וְשֶׁל) יוֹם טוֹב.

Baruch Atah Adonai, Eloheinu melech haolam, asher kid'shanu b'mitzvotav v'tzivanu l'hadlik ner shel [Shabat v'shel] Yom Tov.

Blessed are You, Adonai our God, Sovereign of the world, who made us holy by Your mitzvot, and commanded us to light the [Shabbat and] festival lights.

בָּרוּךְ אַתָּה יי אֱלֹהֵינוּ מֶלֶךְ הָעוֹלָם, שֶׁהֶחֱיָנוּ וְקִיְּמָנוּ וְהִגִּיעָנוּ לַזְּמַן הַזֶּה.

Baruch Atah Adonai, Eloheinu melech haolam, shehecheyanu, v'kiy'manu, v'higiyanu, lazman hazeh.

Blessed are You, Adonai our God, Sovereign of the world, who has kept us alive and sustained us, so we can reach this special occasion.

The Order of the Seder

Jews around the world follow the same order of the seder. The seder contains fourteen parts that we now recite in order.

(If you read or sing the words for the order of the seder in Hebrew, you will see that it is a rhyme. This is a mnemonic device to help us remember what comes next. To introduce each section of the seder, read or sing the song but only to that part.)

KADESH	Sanctifying the wine	קַדֵּשׁ
UR'CHATZ	Washing our hands	וּרְחַץ
KARPAS	Dipping a vegetable in salt water	כַּרְפַּס
YACHATZ	Breaking the middle matzah; Hiding the larger half	יַחַץ
MAGGID	Telling the story	מַגִּיד
RACHTZAH	Washing (with a blessing)	רָחְצָה
MOTZI MATZAH	Eating Matzah	מוֹצִיא מַצָּה
MAROR	Dipping the Bitter Herb	מָרוֹר
KORECH	Eating the Hillel sandwich	כּוֹרֵךְ
SHULCAN ORECH	Eating the Meal	שֻׁלְחָן עוֹרֵךְ
TZAFUN	Tasting the Afikomen	צָפוּן
BARECH	Blessing after the Meal	בָּרֵךְ
HALLEL	Singing Songs of Praise	הַלֵּל
NIRTZAH	Concluding the Seder	נִרְצָה

Seder warm-ups

Ask participants to recall the places where
they have attended a seder.
Have people recall favorite memories of sedarim past.
Stop to remember who may be missing from your seder this year. Share
special memories of that person.
Acknowledge who is at the seder for the first time.

Matzah Making, Bukhara, Uzbekistan, 2000

Wine Cellar, Samarkand, Uzbekistan, 1998

SAY THE KIDDUSH

First Cup – "I Will Take You Out"

(Fill the cups with wine.)

We are now ready for the first cup of wine, which we drink while reclining.
[On Shabbat add the words in brackets.]

(וַיְהִי עֶרֶב וַיְהִי בֹקֶר יוֹם הַשִּׁשִּׁי,

וַיְכֻלּוּ הַשָּׁמַיִם וְהָאָרֶץ וְכָל-צְבָאָם: וַיְכַל אֱלֹהִים בַּיּוֹם הַשְּׁבִיעִי, מְלַאכְתּוֹ אֲשֶׁר עָשָׂה,

וַיִּשְׁבֹּת בַּיּוֹם הַשְּׁבִיעִי, מִכָּל-מְלַאכְתּוֹ אֲשֶׁר עָשָׂה: וַיְבָרֶךְ אֱלֹהִים אֶת-יוֹם הַשְּׁבִיעִי,

וַיְקַדֵּשׁ אֹתוֹ, כִּי בוֹ שָׁבַת מִכָּל-מְלַאכְתּוֹ, אֲשֶׁר-בָּרָא אֱלֹהִים לַעֲשׂוֹת:)

[Vay'hi erev, vay'hi voker yom hashishi: Vay'chulu hashamayim v'ha'aretz v'chol tz'va'am. Vay'chal Elohim bayom hash'vi'i m'lachto asher asah. Vayishbot bayom hash'vi'i mikol m'lachto asher asah. Vay'varech Elohim et yom hash'vi'i vay'kadesh oto, ki vo shavat mikol m'lachto asher bara Elohim la'asot.]

[On the sixth day, the heavens and earth were finished. On the seventh day, God completed the work of creation. God blessed the seventh day and called it holy, because on that day, God rested from all the work of creation.]

בָּרוּךְ אַתָּה יְיָ, אֱלֹהֵינוּ מֶלֶךְ הָעוֹלָם, בּוֹרֵא פְּרִי הַגָּפֶן:

Blessed are You, Adonai our God, Sovereign of the world, who creates the fruit of the vine.

בָּרוּךְ אַתָּה יְיָ, אֱלֹהֵינוּ מֶלֶךְ הָעוֹלָם, אֲשֶׁר בָּחַר בָּנוּ מִכָּל-עָם, וְרוֹמְמָנוּ
מִכָּל-לָשׁוֹן, וְקִדְּשָׁנוּ בְּמִצְוֹתָיו, וַתִּתֶּן-לָנוּ יְיָ אֱלֹהֵינוּ בְּאַהֲבָה (שַׁבָּתוֹת לִמְנוּחָה
וּ)מוֹעֲדִים לְשִׂמְחָה, חַגִּים וּזְמַנִּים לְשָׂשׂוֹן אֶת-יוֹם (הַשַּׁבָּת הַזֶּה וְאֶת-יוֹם) חַג
הַמַּצּוֹת הַזֶּה. זְמַן חֵרוּתֵנוּ, (בְּאַהֲבָה,) מִקְרָא קֹדֶשׁ, זֵכֶר לִיצִיאַת מִצְרָיִם.
כִּי בָנוּ בָחַרְתָּ וְאוֹתָנוּ קִדַּשְׁתָּ מִכָּל-הָעַמִּים. (וְשַׁבָּת) וּמוֹעֲדֵי קָדְשֶׁךָ (בְּאַהֲבָה
וּבְרָצוֹן) בְּשִׂמְחָה וּבְשָׂשׂוֹן הִנְחַלְתָּנוּ. בָּרוּךְ אַתָּה יְיָ, מְקַדֵּשׁ (הַשַּׁבָּת וְ)יִשְׂרָאֵל
וְהַזְּמַנִּים:

Baruch Atah Adonai, Eloheinu melech haolam, asher bachar banu mikol am.
V'rom'manu mikol lashon, v'kidshanu b'mitzvotav. Vatiten lanu Adonai
Eloheinu, b'ahava [Shabbat limnucha u'] mo'adim l'simchah, chagim uz'manim
l'sasson. Et yom [haShabbat hazeh v'et yom] chag hamatzot hazeh, z'man
cherutenu, [b'ahava] mikra kodesh, zecher l'tziat mitzrayim. Ki vanu vaharta,
v'otanu kidashta mikol ha'amim [v'Shabbat] u'mo'adei kadsh'cha [b'ahava]
uv'ratzon, b'simcha uv' sasson hinchaltanu. Baruch Atah Adonai, mikadesh
[haShabbat v'] Yisrael, v'hazmanim.

Blessed are You, Adonai our God, Sovereign of the world, who has made us holy through
your mitzvot, and has lovingly given us the gift of [Shabbat for rest and] festivals for gladness. You have given us [Shabbat and] this Festival of Matzot, celebrations of our freedom,
a holy time to recall the Exodus from Egypt. Blessed are You Adonai, who makes holy
[Shabbat] the people Israel and the festivals.

(On Saturday night, add Havdalah. Note: Passover extends the spirit of Shabbat, so the
blessing for the spices is not recited. The blessing for the light is said over the festival
candles and not over a Havdalah candle.)

Havdalah

בָּרוּךְ אַתָּה יְיָ, אֱלֹהֵינוּ מֶלֶךְ הָעוֹלָם, בּוֹרֵא מְאוֹרֵי הָאֵשׁ:

Baruch Atah Adonai, Eloheinu melech haolam, borei m'orei ha'esh.

Blessed are You, Adonai our God, Sovereign of the world, Creator of light.

בָּרוּךְ אַתָּה יְיָ, אֱלֹהֵינוּ מֶלֶךְ הָעוֹלָם, הַמַּבְדִּיל בֵּין קֹדֶשׁ לְחֹל בֵּין אוֹר לְחֹשֶׁךְ, בֵּין
יִשְׂרָאֵל לָעַמִּים, בֵּין יוֹם הַשְּׁבִיעִי לְשֵׁשֶׁת יְמֵי הַמַּעֲשֶׂה. בֵּין קְדֻשַּׁת שַׁבָּת לִקְדֻשַּׁת
יוֹם טוֹב הִבְדַּלְתָּ. וְאֶת-יוֹם הַשְּׁבִיעִי מִשֵּׁשֶׁת יְמֵי הַמַּעֲשֶׂה קִדַּשְׁתָּ. הִבְדַּלְתָּ וְקִדַּשְׁתָּ
אֶת-עַמְּךָ יִשְׂרָאֵל בִּקְדֻשָּׁתֶךָ. בָּרוּךְ אַתָּה יְיָ, הַמַּבְדִּיל בֵּין קֹדֶשׁ לְקֹדֶשׁ:

Blessed are You, Adonai our God, Sovereign of the world, who separates holy from the profane, light from darkness, Israel from the nations, and Shabbat from the six days of creation. Blessed are You, Adonai, who separates the holiness of Shabbat from the holiness of the festivals.

(continue with the Shehecheyanu prayer)

בָּרוּךְ אַתָּה יְיָ, אֱלֹהֵינוּ מֶלֶךְ הָעוֹלָם, שֶׁהֶחֱיָנוּ וְקִיְּמָנוּ וְהִגִּיעָנוּ לַזְּמַן הַזֶּה:

Baruch Atah Adonai, Eloheinu melech haolam, shehecheyanu, v'ky'manu, v'higiyanu, lazman hazeh.

Blessed are You, Adonai our God, Sovereign of the world, who has kept us alive and sustained us, so that we can reach this special occasion.

(All drink the wine while reclining.)

The seder begins with Kadesh (sanctification), showing that even the physical aspects of our lives can be permeated with holiness.[3]

The kiddush includes the words "simcha" and "sasson," gladness and joy. In Chassidic teaching, the word gladness refers to our happiness over a redemption we have already experienced (the Exodus from Egypt.) Joy, however, refers to a future promise—the Messianic redemption. It is important to note that this theme, of both past and future redemptions, will occur throughout the Haggadah text.

During the course of the seder, we drink four cups of wine which represent God's four promises to the people Israel. (Exodus 6:6-7)
"I will take you out."
"I will rescue you."
"I will redeem you."
"I will take you to be my people."

The Maharal of Prague taught that the expression "I will take you out" refers to intellectual and spiritual exile, while "I will rescue you" refers to physical exile.[4]

Some Jewish feminists associate the four cups of wine at the seder with the four matriarchs of Israel—Sarah, Rebecca, Leah and Rachel. What are characteristics of each matriarch to which you would like to drink a "L'Chaim?"

Have children make paper kiddush cups with the numbers 1, 2, 3, and 4 on them, so they can hold up the appropriate number to show which cup of wine to bless. Challenge them to be awake for all four cups!

WASH OUR HANDS

As the priests in the Holy Temple were commanded to wash, we wash to symbolize that our actions must be of service to God.

(Take a cup of water in one hand and pour it over the other, then reverse hands. You can do this ritual at a sink or bring a cup, bowl, and towel to the table. No blessing is recited.)

Children may carry a cup, a bowl and a towel around to help those washing, or each participant can pour for the one seated next to him or her.

The term "rachatz", which in Hebrew is translated as "to wash", has the meaning "to trust" in Aramaic. According to a Sephardic commentary, washing is an expression of faith and optimism.[5]

Joint Distribution Committee Soup Kitchen, Buenos Aires, Argentina, 2002

DIP A GREEN VEGETABLE

(Distribute the green vegetable.)

We dip a green vegetable into the salt water and recite this blessing:

בָּרוּךְ אַתָּה יְיָ, אֱלֹהֵינוּ מֶלֶךְ הָעוֹלָם, בּוֹרֵא פְּרִי הָאֲדָמָה:

Baruch Atah Adonai, Eloheinu melech haolam, borei p'ri ha'adamah.
Blessed are You, Adonai our God, Sovereign of the world, who creates the fruit of the earth.

(All eat the green vegetable.)

Carnations, Tashkent, Uzbekistan, 2000

The Karpas is usually parsley or celery. In Eastern Europe, potatoes were used because they were more available. Parsley can be grown indoors after Purim to be used at the seder.

In ancient times, like today, an appetizer was served at festive occasions to stimulate the appetite. Karpas is said to stimulate our appetites to eat the required amount of matzah later in the seder. Vegetable hors d'oeuvres and dips can also help hungry children and adults hold out until it is time for the meal to begin.

We dip Karpas into salt water to remember the tears our ancestors shed in the land of Egypt. Another explanation is that this act reminds us that "tears stop when spring comes… and, with it, the potential for change." [6]

Composer and singer, Shlomo Carlebach, taught about the importance of tears: "…I can only tell you that whenever you want to cry, cry with all your heart….But when you cry, do it before the One, the Only One —then suddenly great joy from Heaven will descend into your heart." [7]

Passover is the springtime of the year, the season of renewal. This timing is reflected in Song of Songs, in such verses as these:

> "Arise my beloved; come away my fairest! For the winter is past, the rains are over and gone. The blossoms have appeared on the land; the time of singing has come." (Song of Songs 2:10-12)

Presently, what signs of spring and renewal do you see in the environment, in others, and in yourself?

Put flowers on the table or at each place setting for all to enjoy.

We know it is spring when Passover products appear in the supermarket. Have older participants tell about the foods that were or were not available to them for Pesach in the past.

Some view the Song of Songs as a spring love poem. Others view it as an allegory of the relationship between God and the people Israel. As you pass around the Karpas, sing "Dodi Li," a love song from the Song of Songs or your own favorite love song.

דּוֹדִי לִי וַאֲנִי לוֹ, הָרֹעֶה בַּשׁוֹשַׁנִּים.
מִי זֹאת עוֹלָה מִן הַמִּדְבָּר, מְקֻטֶּרֶת מוֹר וּלְבוֹנָה.

Dodi li va'ani lo, haro'eh bashoshanim. (2x)
Mi zot olah min hamidbar, mi zot olah,
M'kuteret mor, mor u'levonan, mor u'levonan?

My beloved is mine and I am his.
Who is she coming from the desert, in clouds of myrrh and frankincense?

(Song of Songs, 2:16; 3:6)

BREAK THE MIDDLE MATZAH

First, we break the middle matzah into two pieces. Then we wrap the larger piece, the afikomen or dessert matzah, and set it aside. Next, we return the smaller piece to the place with the other two matzot.

(Uncover the matzah plate and raise it for all present to see.)

הָא לַחְמָא עַנְיָא דִּי אֲכָלוּ אַבְהָתָנָא בְּאַרְעָא דְמִצְרָיִם. כָּל דִּכְפִין יֵיתֵי וְיֵכוֹל,
כָּל דִּצְרִיךְ יֵיתֵי וְיִפְסַח. הָשַׁתָּא הָכָא, לְשָׁנָה הַבָּאָה בְּאַרְעָא דְיִשְׂרָאֵל.
הָשַׁתָּא עַבְדֵי, לְשָׁנָה הַבָּאָה בְּנֵי חוֹרִין:

Ha lachma anya di achalu avhatana b'ara d'Mitzraim. Kol dichfin yeitei v'yechol. Kol ditzrich yeitei v'yifsach. Hashatah hacha lashana haba'ah b'ara d' Yisrael. Hashatah avdei l'shanah haba'ah b'nai chorin.

This is the very bread of poverty that our ancestors ate in the land of Egypt. Let all who are hungry come and eat. Let all who are needy come and celebrate Passover with us. Now we celebrate here. Next year, may we celebrate in the land of Israel. Next year, may we be truly free.

(Fill the wine cups for the second time.)

Project Or Soup Kitchen, New York City, USA, 1992

Kitchen, Kiev, Ukraine, 1991

Three Matzot

There are three matzot at the seder to represent the Priests, the Levites, and the Israelites. A Sephardic interpretation is that the top matzah represents "thought", the middle matzah "speech", and the bottom matzah "action." "Speech" is placed in the middle to show that it should be linked to our thoughts and actions.[8]

We break the middle matzah because our redemption is not complete. Pikei Avot (The Ethics of the Fathers) teaches that, "We are not obligated to finish the task, but neither are we free from refraining from beginning."   What do you think is broken in our world and needs repair?

Some set out an extra matzah, a Matzah of Hope, for those Jews who are not free to celebrate Passover. Who in our world do you think is not free?

"This is the very bread of poverty..."

There is a North African custom that before reciting "Let all who are hungry…," the leader takes the seder plate and circles it above the head of each participant while joyfully singing the verse, "In haste we went out of Egypt." This is to indicate that life is a cycle and our fortunes change.[9]

These verses are in Aramaic, the vernacular at the time they were written, to ensure that all would understand the meaning. Today, we can still recite it in Aramaic for its historic value and also in our own tongue to emphasize its importance.

The bread of poverty is more than a symbol of the past. It conveys to us that there is still poverty and suffering in the world. Before Passover, it is customary to make a contribution to organizations that help those in need.

The verse "all who are hungry" can also be defined as people seeking spirituality or community.

If you have decided to include an orange on the seder plate, this is an appropriate time to point to it as a symbol of inclusion. The orange suggests the fruitfulness that results when all kinds of Jews participate fully in the life of the Jewish community.[10]

We add to the joy of the holiday by inviting guests to the seder. It is a mitzvah to include newcomers to the community, college students away from home, or anyone who might be alone.

The seder plate and other rituals prompt children to ask questions. The rabbis of old were consummate educators. They understood that simply telling pieces of information would not necessarily make an impression. Encouraging questions first would be more effective in making the answers more meaningful.

The Four Questions are models to help children get started. They are an intellectual kind of "appetizer." Following the recitation, have the children (and adults) ask other questions they might have about the holiday.

We might give Passover an additional name—"The Festival of Children." We focus on children because they are our sureties, our future. What teachings do you feel are urgently important to transmit to the next generation? What can they teach us?

Think of the first time you asked the Four Questions. Share your memories.[11]

At the time the Haggadah was composed, only the very wealthy would eat reclining on couches rather than sitting on stools or on the ground like the poor. Tonight, we recline on pillows to show that we are "spiritually wealthy" people because of the gift of Torah.

Cave, Haidan A-Sham, Yemen, 1992

TELL THE STORY OF PASSOVER

The Four Questions

(Traditionally, the youngest child asks the Four Questions, but each child could do it in order of birth. Consider having the oldest adult present share the honors with the youngest.)

מַה נִּשְׁתַּנָּה הַלַּיְלָה הַזֶּה מִכָּל הַלֵּילוֹת?

שֶׁבְּכָל הַלֵּילוֹת אָנוּ אוֹכְלִין חָמֵץ וּמַצָּה.
הַלַּיְלָה הַזֶּה כֻּלּוֹ מַצָּה:

שֶׁבְּכָל הַלֵּילוֹת אָנוּ אוֹכְלִין שְׁאָר יְרָקוֹת
הַלַּיְלָה הַזֶּה מָרוֹר:

שֶׁבְּכָל הַלֵּילוֹת אֵין אָנוּ מַטְבִּילִין אֲפִילוּ פַּעַם אֶחָת.
הַלַּיְלָה הַזֶּה שְׁתֵּי פְעָמִים:

שֶׁבְּכָל הַלֵּילוֹת אָנוּ אוֹכְלִין בֵּין יוֹשְׁבִין וּבֵין מְסֻבִּין.
הַלַּיְלָה הַזֶּה כֻּלָּנוּ מְסֻבִּין:

Mah nishtana halailah hazeh mikol haleilot?
Shb'chol haleilot anu ochlin chametz u'matzah. Halaila hazeh kulo matzah.
Shb'chol haleilot anu ochlin sh'ar yerakot. Halailah hazeh maror.
Shb'chol haleilot anu matbilin afilu pa'am echat. Halaila hazeh sh'tei f'amim.
Shb'chol haleilot anu ochlin bein yoshvin u'vein mesubin. Halaila hazeh kulanu m'subin.

Why is this night different from all the other nights of the year?

On all other nights, we eat bread or matzah. On this night, we eat only matzah.

On all other nights, we eat a variety of vegetables. On this night, we must eat maror, a bitter vegetable.

On all other nights, we are not required to dip a vegetable even once. On this night, we must dip twice.

On all other nights, we eat sitting any way we like. On this night, we recline on pillows.

Seedlings, Kibutz Nir David, Israel, 1997

We Were Slaves

עֲבָדִים הָיִינוּ לְפַרְעֹה בְּמִצְרָיִם. וַיּוֹצִיאֵנוּ יְיָ אֱלֹהֵינוּ מִשָּׁם, בְּיָד חֲזָקָה וּבִזְרוֹעַ נְטוּיָה, וְאִלּוּ לֹא הוֹצִיא הַקָּדוֹשׁ בָּרוּךְ הוּא אֶת־אֲבוֹתֵינוּ מִמִּצְרָיִם, הֲרֵי אָנוּ וּבָנֵינוּ וּבְנֵי בָנֵינוּ, מְשֻׁעְבָּדִים הָיִינוּ לְפַרְעֹה בְּמִצְרָיִם. וַאֲפִילוּ כֻּלָּנוּ חֲכָמִים, כֻּלָּנוּ נְבוֹנִים, כֻּלָּנוּ זְקֵנִים, כֻּלָּנוּ יוֹדְעִים אֶת־הַתּוֹרָה, מִצְוָה עָלֵינוּ לְסַפֵּר בִּיצִיאַת מִצְרָיִם. וְכָל הַמַּרְבֶּה לְסַפֵּר בִּיצִיאַת מִצְרָיִם, הֲרֵי זֶה מְשֻׁבָּח:

Avadim haiyenu, atah b'nai chorin.

Once we were slaves to the Pharaoh in Egypt and Adonai, our God, took us out, "with a mighty hand and an outstretched arm." If the Holy One of Blessing had not brought our ancestors out of Egypt, then we and our descendants would still be enslaved in Egypt. Even if we were all wise, or all full of understanding, or we were all elders who had told the story numerous times, or all Torah scholars, it is still our duty to tell the story. The more we expand upon the story, the more we are to be praised.

Honorable Discharge, Russian Immigrants, Israel, 1992

When it is time to recite "We Were Slaves…," a Bukharian custom is for the seder leader to get up and walk around in a bent position, as if he or she were a slave. Have the children do this or other pantomimes to depict slavery.[12]

This reading does not specifically answer the Four Questions. It is not really a narrative, but a declaration as to why we are all obligated to tell the story of the Exodus and express gratitude for our deliverance.

How does knowing that we were once slaves help us understand how we should act towards others?

What does the poet Emma Lazarus mean when she says that, "Until all of us are free, none of us is free?"

What kinds of slavery are practiced in the world today? Do you think we are moving in the direction of greater or lesser freedom in our country and throughout the world?

Share something that is "enslaving" that you would like to change in your life.

Children's Song

Bang and Dig

Bang, bang, bang,
Bang your hammers low.
Bang, bang, bang,
Give a heavy blow.

Chorus
'Cause it's work, work, work,
Every day and every night,
'Cause it's work, work, work,
When it's dark
and when it's light.

Did, dig, dig,
Dig your shovels deep.
Dig, dig, dig,
There's no time for sleep

Repeat chorus

Recess at Jewish Day School, Djerba, Tunisia, 1995

The B'nai B'rak Story

While reading the Haggadah is mandatory, elaborating upon it is praiseworthy. We are shown an example of this in the B'nai B'rak story.

An incident happened with Rabbi Eliezer, Rabbi Yehoshua, Rabbi Elazar ben Azaryah, Rabbi Akiva and Rabbi Tarfon. They were celebrating at a seder in B'nai B'rak and were recounting the story of the Exodus from Egypt all through the night. Their students came and interrupted them saying, "Our rabbis, the time has come for reciting the morning Shema!"

מַעֲשֶׂה בְּרַבִּי אֱלִיעֶזֶר, וְרַבִּי יְהוֹשֻעַ, וְרַבִּי אֶלְעָזָר בֶּן־עֲזַרְיָה, וְרַבִּי עֲקִיבָא, וְרַבִּי טַרְפוֹן, שֶׁהָיוּ מְסֻבִּין בִּבְנֵי־בְרַק, וְהָיוּ מְסַפְּרִים בִּיצִיאַת מִצְרַיִם, כָּל־אוֹתוֹ הַלַּיְלָה, עַד שֶׁבָּאוּ תַלְמִידֵיהֶם וְאָמְרוּ לָהֶם: רַבּוֹתֵינוּ, הִגִּיעַ זְמַן קְרִיאַת שְׁמַע, שֶׁל שַׁחֲרִית:

אָמַר רַבִּי אֶלְעָזָר בֶּן־עֲזַרְיָה. הֲרֵי אֲנִי כְּבֶן שִׁבְעִים שָׁנָה, וְלֹא זָכִיתִי, שֶׁתֵּאָמֵר יְצִיאַת מִצְרַיִם בַּלֵּילוֹת. עַד שֶׁדְּרָשָׁהּ בֶּן זוֹמָא. שֶׁנֶּאֱמַר: לְמַעַן תִּזְכֹּר, אֶת יוֹם צֵאתְךָ מֵאֶרֶץ מִצְרַיִם, כֹּל יְמֵי חַיֶּיךָ. יְמֵי חַיֶּיךָ הַיָּמִים. כֹּל יְמֵי חַיֶּיךָ הַלֵּילוֹת. וַחֲכָמִים אוֹמְרִים: יְמֵי חַיֶּיךָ הָעוֹלָם הַזֶּה. כֹּל יְמֵי חַיֶּיךָ לְהָבִיא לִימוֹת הַמָּשִׁיחַ:

Sunrise, Sde Boker, Israel 2003

Some have interpreted this story as a gathering to support the Bar Kochba rebellion in 132 C.E. against the Roman Empire. Hiding in a cave, the supporters were so engrossed in discussion that they did not realize that the time had come to say the morning Shema. Give examples of other small groups that met to fight tyranny.

Since both Rabbi Joshua and Rabbi Eliezer died before the revolt, this account would not be likely historically. Another interpretation is to view this story as a mythical seder created to reunite the great sages Rabbis Azariah, Tarfon, and Akiba with Rabbi Eliezer from whom they had distanced themselves. Rabbi Eliezer's unwillingness to accept a ruling of the High Court was the impetus for this estrangement. At this mythical seder, their broken relationship was mended. All opinions were expressed, including Rabbi Eliezer's.14 This legend teaches us NOT to exclude anyone from participating in the seder or other Jewish communal events, even when their views are unpopular.

Who in the Jewish community would you say is excluded today?

How can we bring more Jews to the seder table?

The One Who Is Everywhere

Once we worshipped idols, but now we worship God, the One Who Is Everywhere.

בָּרוּךְ הַמָּקוֹם. בָּרוּךְ הוּא.
בָּרוּךְ שֶׁנָּתַן תּוֹרָה לְעַמּוֹ יִשְׂרָאֵל. בָּרוּךְ הוּא.

***Baruch HaMakom. Baruch Hu. Baruch Shenatan Torah l'amo Yisrael.
Baruch Hu.***

Blessed is The One Who Is Everywhere. Blessed is God. Blessed is the One who gave the Torah to the people Israel. Blessed is God.

A Scribe, Mumbai, (Bombay), India, 2001

The Hebrew text literally says "Blessed is The Place". God is referred to as "The Place" to teach that there is no place that is devoid of God's presence.

Calling God "The Place" makes us see God as a destination, the end of a spiritual journey.[13]

Where do you feel you are on this journey?

The text "Blessed is the One who gave the Torah" is inserted here to acknowledge that our liberation from Egypt gave us the opportunity to accept the Torah at Sinai.

Four Children, Maimonides School, Santiago, Chile, 2002

The Four Children

The Torah addresses itself to four children: the wise, the wicked, the simple, and one who does not know how to ask.

What does the wise child ask? "What is the meaning of the laws and rules which our God has commanded us?" (Deuteronomy 6:20) You should explain to that child all the laws of Passover, including the rule that nothing may be eaten after the afikomen.

What does the wicked child ask? "What does this service mean to you?" (Exodus 12:26) (Implying "to you" and not "to him or her.") Since this child excludes him/ herself from the rest of the community, you answer in a shocking manner, "I celebrate Passover because of what God did for me when I went out of Egypt." (Exodus 13:8) If the wicked child had been in Egypt, he or she would have not been included in the redemption.

What does the simple child ask? "What is this?" You answer: "With a mighty hand, God took us out of Egypt, out of slavery." (Exodus 13:14)

As for the one who does not know how to ask, you must introduce the subject yourself, as it says, "You shall tell your child on that day, it is because of what God did for me when I left Egypt." (Exodus 13:8)

כְּנֶגֶד אַרְבָּעָה בָנִים דִּבְּרָה תוֹרָה. אֶחָד חָכָם, וְאֶחָד רָשָׁע, וְאֶחָד תָּם, וְאֶחָד שֶׁאֵינוֹ יוֹדֵעַ לִשְׁאוֹל:

חָכָם מַה הוּא אוֹמֵר? מָה הָעֵדֹת וְהַחֻקִּים וְהַמִּשְׁפָּטִים, אֲשֶׁר צִוָּה יְיָ אֱלֹהֵינוּ אֶתְכֶם? וְאַף אַתָּה אֱמָר־לוֹ כְּהִלְכוֹת הַפֶּסַח: אֵין מַפְטִירִין אַחַר הַפֶּסַח אֲפִיקוֹמָן:

רָשָׁע מַה הוּא אוֹמֵר? מָה הָעֲבֹדָה הַזֹּאת לָכֶם? לָכֶם וְלֹא לוֹ. וּלְפִי שֶׁהוֹצִיא אֶת־עַצְמוֹ מִן הַכְּלָל, כָּפַר בָּעִקָּר. וְאַף אַתָּה הַקְהֵה אֶת־שִׁנָּיו, וֶאֱמָר־לוֹ: בַּעֲבוּר זֶה, עָשָׂה יְיָ לִי, בְּצֵאתִי מִמִּצְרַיִם, לִי וְלֹא־לוֹ. אִלּוּ הָיָה שָׁם, לֹא הָיָה נִגְאָל:

תָּם מַה הוּא אוֹמֵר? מַה זֹּאת? וְאָמַרְתָּ אֵלָיו: בְּחֹזֶק יָד הוֹצִיאָנוּ יְיָ מִמִּצְרַיִם מִבֵּית עֲבָדִים:

וְשֶׁאֵינוֹ יוֹדֵעַ לִשְׁאוֹל, אַתְּ פְּתַח לוֹ. שֶׁנֶּאֱמַר: וְהִגַּדְתָּ לְבִנְךָ, בַּיּוֹם הַהוּא לֵאמֹר: בַּעֲבוּר זֶה עָשָׂה יְיָ לִי, בְּצֵאתִי מִמִּצְרָיִם:

יָכוֹל מֵרֹאשׁ חֹדֶשׁ, תַּלְמוּד לוֹמַר בַּיּוֹם הַהוּא. אִי בַּיּוֹם הַהוּא. יָכוֹל מִבְּעוֹד יוֹם. תַּלְמוּד לוֹמַר. בַּעֲבוּר זֶה. בַּעֲבוּר זֶה לֹא אָמַרְתִּי, אֶלָּא בְּשָׁעָה שֶׁיֵּשׁ מַצָּה וּמָרוֹר מֻנָּחִים לְפָנֶיךָ:

Mother and Son, Absorption Center, Hadera, Israel, 1998

For teaching to be effective, it must be varied so that each person receives it on his or her own level. Do you think the Haggadah text does this successfully or not?

At first glance, the wise child receives a short, dry response to a profound, soul-searching question. He or she is taught about not eating food after the afikomen. On a deeper level, the response is a spiritual teaching: that the sacred (the lingering taste of the dessert matzah) must remain in our consciousness, so that it becomes a vital part of our being. [15]

Do you think the wicked child is feeling disengaged, or making a challenging declaration, or using the occasion to start an argument, or testing our limits or asking a sincere question?

The traditional response to the wicked child is harsh because this child is said to have separated him/herself from the community and therefore does not share in its fate.[16] At what point, if any, do you think someone should be cut off from the Jewish community?

The "Tam" is usually translated as the "simple" or "naïve" child, but can also be translated as "whole" or "perfect" . . . one with uncomplicated faith. Which translation do you prefer?

Sometimes, we shortchange children with special needs by giving only simple answers and not having higher expectations. Is this happening with the "Tam?"

Why can't the last child ("sh'aino yodea lishol") ask a question?

There are aspects of all four children in each of us. Share a time you felt like each one.

Which children are missing from this reading?

Can you rewrite this part of the Haggadah so it is about the "Four Parents?"

Mother and Son, Operation Solomon, Ben Gurion Airport, Israel, 1991

The Story of Passover

Our story begins with the patriarchs and matriarchs of old—Abraham and Sarah, Isaac and Rebecca, Jacob, Leah and Rachel. God made a covenant with them, promising that their descendants would be as numerous as the stars and that they would become a great nation. But first, their descendants would sojourn in a foreign land for four hundred years where they would be enslaved and finally set free. Then, God said, the Israelites would return to the land of their ancestors. This indeed occurred.

The sojourn to Egypt came about because the jealous brothers of Joseph, the favorite son of the patriarch Jacob, sold him into slavery. Joseph was taken to Egypt. Eventually, he became an advisor to the Pharaoh because of his ability to interpret

[Traditional Text]

מִתְּחִלָּה עוֹבְדֵי עֲבוֹדָה זָרָה הָיוּ אֲבוֹתֵינוּ.
וְעַכְשָׁו קֵרְבָנוּ הַמָּקוֹם לַעֲבוֹדָתוֹ. שֶׁנֶּאֱמַר:
וַיֹּאמֶר יְהוֹשֻׁעַ אֶל־כָּל־הָעָם. כֹּה אָמַר יְיָ
אֱלֹהֵי יִשְׂרָאֵל, בְּעֵבֶר הַנָּהָר יָשְׁבוּ אֲבוֹתֵיכֶם
מֵעוֹלָם, תֶּרַח אֲבִי אַבְרָהָם וַאֲבִי נָחוֹר.
וַיַּעַבְדוּ אֱלֹהִים אֲחֵרִים: וָאֶקַח אֶת־אֲבִיכֶם
אֶת־אַבְרָהָם מֵעֵבֶר הַנָּהָר, וָאוֹלֵךְ אוֹתוֹ
בְּכָל־אֶרֶץ כְּנָעַן. וָאַרְבֶּה אֶת־זַרְעוֹ, וָאֶתֶּן
לוֹ אֶת־יִצְחָק: וָאֶתֵּן לְיִצְחָק אֶת־יַעֲקֹב וְאֶת־
עֵשָׂו. וָאֶתֵּן לְעֵשָׂו אֶת־הַר שֵׂעִיר, לָרֶשֶׁת
אוֹתוֹ. וְיַעֲקֹב וּבָנָיו יָרְדוּ מִצְרָיִם:

בָּרוּךְ שׁוֹמֵר הַבְטָחָתוֹ לְיִשְׂרָאֵל. בָּרוּךְ
הוּא. שֶׁהַקָּדוֹשׁ בָּרוּךְ הוּא חִשַּׁב אֶת־הַקֵּץ,
לַעֲשׂוֹת כְּמָה שֶׁאָמַר לְאַבְרָהָם אָבִינוּ
בִּבְרִית בֵּין הַבְּתָרִים, שֶׁנֶּאֱמַר: וַיֹּאמֶר
לְאַבְרָם יָדֹעַ תֵּדַע, כִּי־גֵר יִהְיֶה זַרְעֲךָ,
בְּאֶרֶץ לֹא לָהֶם, וַעֲבָדוּם וְעִנּוּ אֹתָם אַרְבַּע
מֵאוֹת שָׁנָה: וְגַם אֶת־הַגּוֹי אֲשֶׁר יַעֲבֹדוּ דָן

dreams. Joseph instructed Pharaoh to build storehouses for grain to feed the people during seven years of famine that would follow seven years of plenty.

When famine came as predicted, Joseph's brothers traveled to Egypt to purchase food. Joseph revealed himself to them and invited his whole family to settle there. Here in Egypt, Jacob's household multiplied and lived peacefully for many years, until a new Pharaoh arose "who knew not Joseph" and did not remember his wise counsel. This Pharaoh feared that the Hebrews would become too numerous and join his enemies to fight against him.

The new Pharaoh decided to make the Hebrews slaves, forcing them to do harsh labor. They were assigned to build garrison cities with bricks made from clay and straw. However, the more the Hebrews were oppressed, the more they increased. Pharaoh then decreed that all male babies

אָנֹכִי. וְאַחֲרֵי כֵן יֵצְאוּ, בִּרְכֻשׁ גָּדוֹל:

(מכסים את המצות ומגביהים את הכוס)

וְהִיא שֶׁעָמְדָה לַאֲבוֹתֵינוּ וְלָנוּ. שֶׁלֹּא אֶחָד בִּלְבָד, עָמַד עָלֵינוּ לְכַלּוֹתֵנוּ. אֶלָּא שֶׁבְּכָל דּוֹר וָדוֹר, עוֹמְדִים עָלֵינוּ לְכַלּוֹתֵנוּ. וְהַקָּדוֹשׁ בָּרוּךְ הוּא מַצִּילֵנוּ מִיָּדָם:

צֵא וּלְמַד, מַה בִּקֵּשׁ לָבָן הָאֲרַמִּי לַעֲשׂוֹת לְיַעֲקֹב אָבִינוּ. שֶׁפַּרְעֹה לֹא גָזַר אֶלָּא עַל הַזְּכָרִים, וְלָבָן בִּקֵּשׁ לַעֲקֹר אֶת־הַכֹּל, שֶׁנֶּאֱמַר: אֲרַמִּי אֹבֵד אָבִי, וַיֵּרֶד מִצְרַיְמָה, וַיָּגָר שָׁם בִּמְתֵי מְעָט.וַיְהִי שָׁם לְגוֹי גָּדוֹל, עָצוּם וָרָב:

וַיֵּרֶד מִצְרַיְמָה, אָנוּס עַל פִּי הַדִּבּוּר. וַיָּגָר שָׁם. מְלַמֵּד שֶׁלֹּא יָרַד יַעֲקֹב אָבִינוּ לְהִשְׁתַּקֵּעַ בְּמִצְרַיִם, אֶלָּא לָגוּר שָׁם, שֶׁנֶּאֱמַר: וַיֹּאמְרוּ אֶל־פַּרְעֹה, לָגוּר בָּאָרֶץ בָּאנוּ, כִּי אֵין מִרְעֶה לַצֹּאן אֲשֶׁר לַעֲבָדֶיךָ, כִּי כָבֵד הָרָעָב בְּאֶרֶץ כְּנָעַן. וְעַתָּה, יֵשְׁבוּ־נָא עֲבָדֶיךָ בְּאֶרֶץ גֹּשֶׁן:

בִּמְתֵי מְעָט. כְּמָה שֶׁנֶּאֱמַר: בְּשִׁבְעִים נֶפֶשׁ,

Circumcision Ceremony, Bukhara, Uzbekistan, 1993

be killed. The midwives, Shifra and Puah, fearing God, defied Pharaoh and let them live. Their clever ruse was to report that the Hebrew women were too vigorous and gave birth before they arrived. Seeing his evil plan thwarted, Pharaoh then decreed "Every boy that is born, you shall throw him into the Nile."

One Hebrew mother, Yocheved, feared she could no longer hide her baby. She made the heart-rending decision to place the baby into a basket to float on the river. The child's older sister Miriam hid in the reeds to watch. She observed the Pharaoh's daughter bathing in the Nile. When the princess heard the infant crying, she took pity on him. Defying her father's cruel decree, she rescued the helpless baby. She named him "Moshe" (Moses), meaning "drawn from the water" and adopted him as her own. Miriam bravely stepped forward offering to find a nurse for the child. When Pharaoh's daughter agreed, she ran to fetch Yocheved. Although Moses was raised in the royal palace, the Torah tells us nothing of his childhood. The story continues with Moses as a man.

Once, when Moses saw an Egyptian task-master beating a Hebrew slave, he could not control his anger and killed him. When he learned that his action was known, he feared for his life and fled to the land of Midian. Here he saved the seven daughters of the Midianite priest Jethro from some rowdy shepherds. His good deed brought him to dwell in Jethro's household and marry Tzipporah, one of his daughters, with whom he had two sons. Moses became a shepherd and tended his father-in-law's flock.

There is a legend that once, when Moses

יָרְדוּ אֲבֹתֶיךָ מִצְרָיְמָה. וְעַתָּה, שָׂמְךָ יְיָ אֱלֹהֶיךָ, כְּכוֹכְבֵי הַשָּׁמַיִם לָרֹב.

וַיְהִי שָׁם לְגוֹי. מְלַמֵּד שֶׁהָיוּ יִשְׂרָאֵל מְצֻיָּנִים שָׁם:

גָּדוֹל עָצוּם, כְּמָה שֶׁנֶּאֱמַר: וּבְנֵי יִשְׂרָאֵל, פָּרוּ וַיִּשְׁרְצוּ, וַיִּרְבּוּ וַיַּעַצְמוּ, בִּמְאֹד מְאֹד, וַתִּמָּלֵא הָאָרֶץ אֹתָם:

וָרָב. כְּמָה שֶׁנֶּאֱמַר: רְבָבָה כְּצֶמַח הַשָּׂדֶה נְתַתִּיךְ, וַתִּרְבִּי, וַתִּגְדְּלִי, וַתָּבֹאִי בַּעֲדִי עֲדָיִים: שָׁדַיִם נָכֹנוּ, וּשְׂעָרֵךְ צִמֵּחַ, וְאַתְּ עֵרֹם וְעֶרְיָה:

וָאֶעֱבֹר עָלַיִךְ וָאֶרְאֵךְ מִתְבּוֹסֶסֶת בְּדָמָיִךְ וָאֹמַר לָךְ בְּדָמַיִךְ חֲיִי וָאֹמַר לָךְ בְּדָמַיִךְ חֲיִי.

וַיָּרֵעוּ אֹתָנוּ הַמִּצְרִים וַיְעַנּוּנוּ. וַיִּתְּנוּ עָלֵינוּ עֲבֹדָה קָשָׁה: וַיָּרֵעוּ אֹתָנוּ הַמִּצְרִים. כְּמָה שֶׁנֶּאֱמַר:הָבָה נִתְחַכְּמָה לוֹ. פֶּן־יִרְבֶּה, וְהָיָה כִּי־תִקְרֶאנָה מִלְחָמָה, וְנוֹסַף גַּם הוּא עַל־שֹׂנְאֵינוּ, וְנִלְחַם־בָּנוּ וְעָלָה מִן־הָאָרֶץ:

וַיְעַנּוּנוּ. כְּמָה שֶׁנֶּאֱמַר: וַיָּשִׂימוּ עָלָיו שָׂרֵי מִסִּים, לְמַעַן עַנֹּתוֹ בְּסִבְלֹתָם: וַיִּבֶן עָרֵי מִסְכְּנוֹת לְפַרְעֹה, אֶת־פִּתֹם וְאֶת־רַעַמְסֵס: וַיִּתְּנוּ עָלֵינוּ עֲבֹדָה קָשָׁה. כְּמָה שֶׁנֶּאֱמַר: וַיַּעֲבִדוּ מִצְרַיִם אֶת־בְּנֵי יִשְׂרָאֵל בְּפָרֶךְ:
וַנִּצְעַק אֶל־יְיָ אֱלֹהֵי אֲבֹתֵינוּ, וַיִּשְׁמַע יְיָ אֶת־קֹלֵנוּ, וַיַּרְא אֶת־עָנְיֵנוּ, וְאֶת־עֲמָלֵנוּ, וְאֶת־לַחֲצֵנוּ: וַנִּצְעַק אֶל־יְיָ אֱלֹהֵי אֲבֹתֵינוּ, כְּמָה שֶׁנֶּאֱמַר: וַיְהִי בַיָּמִים הָרַבִּים הָהֵם, וַיָּמָת מֶלֶךְ מִצְרַיִם, וַיֵּאָנְחוּ בְנֵי־יִשְׂרָאֵל מִן הָעֲבֹדָה וַיִּזְעָקוּ. וַתַּעַל שַׁוְעָתָם אֶל־הָאֱלֹהִים מִן־הָעֲבֹדָה:

וַיִּשְׁמַע יְיָ אֶת־קֹלֵנוּ. כְּמָה שֶׁנֶּאֱמַר: וַיִּשְׁמַע אֱלֹהִים אֶת־נַאֲקָתָם, וַיִּזְכֹּר אֱלֹהִים אֶת־בְּרִיתוֹ, אֶת־אַבְרָהָם, אֶת־יִצְחָק, וְאֶת־יַעֲקֹב:

וַיַּרְא אֶת־עָנְיֵנוּ: זוֹ פְּרִישׁוּת דֶּרֶךְ אֶרֶץ. כְּמָה שֶׁנֶּאֱמַר: וַיַּרְא אֱלֹהִים אֶת־בְּנֵי יִשְׂרָאֵל. וַיֵּדַע אֱלֹהִים:

was tending the sheep, a little lamb strayed from the flock. Though tired from the long day, Moses searched until he found the lamb and tenderly carried it back to the flock. God saw this loving act and decided that someone who cared so much for this little lamb would surely take good care of the "flock of Israel."

While tending sheep on Mount Horeb, God appeared to Moses in a burning bush that was not consumed. From the bush, God's voice called to him saying, "I am the God of your ancestors. I have seen the suffering of the people Israel and have heard their cries. I am ready to take them out of Egypt and bring them to a new land, one that is flowing with milk and honey."

God then told Moses to return to Egypt to bring the message of freedom to the Hebrews and to warn Pharaoh to let the slaves go or suffer terrible consequences. The humble Moses tried five times to refuse, believing that the Hebrews would not accept him as God's messenger, nor would Pharaoh listen to him.

"I will be with you" God promised, and gave Moses the words to convince the Hebrews that he was God's messenger and the signs to demonstrate God's power to Pharaoh. God also assured Moses, who described himself as being "slow of speech and slow of tongue", that his older brother Aaron could be his "mouthpiece." With these assurances, Moses said farewell to Jethro, who told him to go in peace. Then he set out for Egypt.

With Aaron by his side, Moses became the leader of the Hebrews. He returned to his childhood home to confront the Pharaoh. The signs and wonders Moses performed

וְאֶת־עֲמָלֵנוּ.אֵלוּ הַבָּנִים. כְּמָה שֶׁנֶּאֱמַר: כָּל־הַבֵּן הַיִּלּוֹד הַיְאֹרָה תַּשְׁלִיכֻהוּ, וְכָל־הַבַּת תְּחַיּוּן:

וְאֶת לַחֲצֵנוּ. זֶה הַדְּחַק. כְּמָה שֶׁנֶּאֱמַר: וְגַם־רָאִיתִי אֶת־הַלַּחַץ, אֲשֶׁר מִצְרַיִם לֹחֲצִים אֹתָם:

וַיּוֹצִאֵנוּ יְיָ מִמִּצְרַיִם, בְּיָד חֲזָקָה, וּבִזְרֹעַ נְטוּיָה, וּבְמֹרָא גָּדֹל וּבְאֹתוֹת וּבְמֹפְתִים:

וַיּוֹצִאֵנוּ יְיָ מִמִּצְרַיִם. לֹא עַל־יְדֵי מַלְאָךְ, וְלֹא עַל־יְדֵי שָׂרָף, וְלֹא עַל־יְדֵי שָׁלִיחַ. אֶלָּא הַקָּדוֹשׁ בָּרוּךְ הוּא בִּכְבוֹדוֹ וּבְעַצְמוֹ. שֶׁנֶּאֱמַר: וְעָבַרְתִּי בְאֶרֶץ מִצְרַיִם בַּלַּיְלָה הַזֶּה, וְהִכֵּיתִי כָל־בְּכוֹר בְּאֶרֶץ מִצְרַיִם, מֵאָדָם וְעַד בְּהֵמָה, וּבְכָל־אֱלֹהֵי מִצְרַיִם אֶעֱשֶׂה שְׁפָטִים אֲנִי יְיָ:

וְעָבַרְתִּי בְאֶרֶץ־מִצְרַיִם בַּלַּיְלָה הַזֶּה, אֲנִי וְלֹא מַלְאָךְ. וְהִכֵּיתִי כָל־בְּכוֹר בְּאֶרֶץ־מִצְרַיִם. אֲנִי וְלֹא שָׂרָף. וּבְכָל־אֱלֹהֵי מִצְרַיִם אֶעֱשֶׂה שְׁפָטִים, אֲנִי וְלֹא הַשָּׁלִיחַ. אֲנִי יְיָ. אֲנִי הוּא וְלֹא אַחֵר:

בְּיָד חֲזָקָה. זוֹ הַדֶּבֶר. כְּמָה שֶׁנֶּאֱמַר: הִנֵּה יַד־יְיָ הוֹיָה, בְּמִקְנְךָ אֲשֶׁר בַּשָּׂדֶה, בַּסּוּסִים בַּחֲמֹרִים בַּגְּמַלִּים, בַּבָּקָר וּבַצֹּאן, דֶּבֶר כָּבֵד מְאֹד:

וּבִזְרֹעַ נְטוּיָה. זוֹ הַחֶרֶב. כְּמָה שֶׁנֶּאֱמַר: וְחַרְבּוֹ שְׁלוּפָה בְּיָדוֹ, נְטוּיָה עַל־יְרוּשָׁלָיִם:

וּבְמֹרָא גָּדֹל, זֶה גִּלּוּי שְׁכִינָה. כְּמָה שֶׁנֶּאֱמַר: אוֹ הֲנִסָּה אֱלֹהִים, לָבוֹא לָקַחַת לוֹ גוֹי מִקֶּרֶב גּוֹי, בְּמַסֹּת בְּאֹתֹת וּבְמוֹפְתִים וּבְמִלְחָמָה, וּבְיָד חֲזָקָה וּבִזְרוֹעַ נְטוּיָה, וּבְמוֹרָאִים גְּדֹלִים. כְּכֹל אֲשֶׁר־עָשָׂה לָכֶם יְיָ אֱלֹהֵיכֶם בְּמִצְרַיִם, לְעֵינֶיךָ:

וּבְאֹתוֹת. זֶה הַמַּטֶּה. כְּמָה שֶׁנֶּאֱמַר: וְאֶת הַמַּטֶּה הַזֶּה תִּקַּח בְּיָדֶךָ. אֲשֶׁר תַּעֲשֶׂה־בּוֹ אֶת־הָאֹתֹת:

וּבְמֹפְתִים. זֶה הַדָּם. כְּמָה שֶׁנֶּאֱמַר: וְנָתַתִּי

Shepherd, Kfar Zetim, Israel, 1984

did not impress Pharaoh and he refused to comply. He forced the Hebrews to work even harder, making their own straw for the bricks they needed for building. God, as promised, brought ten plagues on the Egyptians. Even the suffering of his own people did not move Pharaoh. Although frightened, Pharaoh was stubborn. He said he would let the Hebrews go, but kept changing his mind. Pharaoh did not relent until the final plague, the slaying of the first born in all of Egypt, included his own household. This convinced Pharaoh to let them go!

מוֹפְתִים, בַּשָּׁמַיִם וּבָאָרֶץ

(נוהגים להטיף מעט מן הכוס בעת אמירת דם ואש, וגם באמירת דם צפרדע, וכו', וגם באמירת דצ"ך עד"ש וכו')

דָּם. וָאֵשׁ. וְתִימְרוֹת עָשָׁן:

דָּבָר אַחֵר. בְּיָד חֲזָקָה שְׁתַּיִם. וּבִזְרֹעַ נְטוּיָה שְׁתַּיִם. וּבְמוֹרָא גָּדוֹל שְׁתַּיִם. וּבְאֹתוֹת שְׁתַּיִם. וּבְמוֹפְתִים שְׁתַּיִם:אֵלּוּ עֶשֶׂר מַכּוֹת שֶׁהֵבִיא הַקָּדוֹשׁ בָּרוּךְ הוּא עַל־הַמִּצְרִים בְּמִצְרַיִם, וְאֵלּוּ הֵן:

The Ten Plagues

We now fill our wine cups to remember our great joy in being able to leave Egypt, yet our happiness is diminished because the Egyptians, who are also God's children, suffered because of Pharaoh's hardness of heart and cruel leadership. Therefore, we spill a drop of wine from our own cups (with a finger or a spoon) as we recite each plague.

Blood	*Dam*	דָּם
Frogs	*Tz'fardaiya*	צְפַרְדֵּעַ
Lice	*Kinim*	כִּנִּים
Beasts	*Arov*	עָרוֹב
Cattle Disease	*Dever*	דֶּבֶר
Boils	*Sh'chin*	שְׁחִין
Hail	*Barad*	בָּרָד
Locusts	*Arbeh*	אַרְבֶּה
Darkness	*Choshech*	חֹשֶׁךְ
Plague of the Firstborn	*Makat B'chorot*	מַכַּת בְּכוֹרוֹת

Blessings for the Circumcised, Mexico City, Mexico, 2004

[Traditional Text]

רַבִּי יְהוּדָה הָיָה נוֹתֵן בָּהֶם סִמָּנִים:
דְּצַ"ךְ עַד"שׁ בְּאַחַ"ב:

רַבִּי יוֹסֵי הַגְּלִילִי אוֹמֵר: מִנַּיִן אַתָּה אוֹמֵר,
שֶׁלָּקוּ הַמִּצְרִים בְּמִצְרַיִם עֶשֶׂר מַכּוֹת, וְעַל
הַיָּם, לָקוּ חֲמִשִּׁים מַכּוֹת? בְּמִצְרַיִם מָה הוּא
אוֹמֵר: וַיֹּאמְרוּ הַחַרְטֻמִּם אֶל־פַּרְעֹה, אֶצְבַּע
אֱלֹהִים הוּא. וְעַל הַיָּם מָה הוּא אוֹמֵר? וַיַּרְא
יִשְׂרָאֵל אֶת־הַיָּד הַגְּדֹלָה, אֲשֶׁר עָשָׂה יְיָ
בְּמִצְרַיִם, וַיִּירְאוּ הָעָם אֶת־יְיָ. וַיַּאֲמִינוּ בַּיְיָ,
וּבְמֹשֶׁה עַבְדּוֹ. כַּמָּה לָקוּ בְּאֶצְבַּע, עֶשֶׂר
מַכּוֹת: אֱמוֹר מֵעַתָּה, בְּמִצְרַיִם לָקוּ עֶשֶׂר
מַכּוֹת, וְעַל־הַיָּם, לָקוּ חֲמִשִּׁים מַכּוֹת:

רַבִּי אֱלִיעֶזֶר אוֹמֵר: מִנַּיִן שֶׁכָּל־מַכָּה וּמַכָּה,
שֶׁהֵבִיא הַקָּדוֹשׁ בָּרוּךְ הוּא עַל הַמִּצְרִים

בְּמִצְרַיִם, הָיְתָה שֶׁל אַרְבַּע מַכּוֹת? שֶׁנֶּאֱמַר:
יְשַׁלַּח־בָּם חֲרוֹן אַפּוֹ, עֶבְרָה וָזַעַם וְצָרָה.
מִשְׁלַחַת מַלְאֲכֵי רָעִים. עֶבְרָה אַחַת. וָזַעַם
שְׁתַּיִם. וְצָרָה שָׁלֹשׁ. מִשְׁלַחַת מַלְאֲכֵי רָעִים
אַרְבַּע: אֱמוֹר מֵעַתָּה, בְּמִצְרַיִם לָקוּ אַרְבָּעִים
מַכּוֹת, וְעַל הַיָּם לָקוּ מָאתַיִם מַכּוֹת:

רַבִּי עֲקִיבָא אוֹמֵר: מִנַּיִן שֶׁכָּל־מַכָּה וּמַכָּה,
שֶׁהֵבִיא הַקָּדוֹשׁ בָּרוּךְ הוּא עַל הַמִּצְרַיִם
בְּמִצְרַיִם, הָיְתָה שֶׁל חָמֵשׁ מַכּוֹת? שֶׁנֶּאֱמַר:
יְשַׁלַּח־בָּם חֲרוֹן אַפּוֹ, עֶבְרָה וָזַעַם וְצָרָה.
מִשְׁלַחַת מַלְאֲכֵי רָעִים. חֲרוֹן אַפּוֹ אַחַת.
עֶבְרָה שְׁתַּיִם. וָזַעַם שָׁלֹשׁ. וְצָרָה אַרְבַּע.
מִשְׁלַחַת מַלְאֲכֵי רָעִים חָמֵשׁ : אֱמוֹר
מֵעַתָּה, בְּמִצְרַיִם לָקוּ חֲמִשִּׁים מַכּוֹת, וְעַל
הַיָּם לָקוּ חֲמִשִּׁים וּמָאתַיִם מַכּוֹת:

CROSSING THE SEA TO FREEDOM

Soon after Pharaoh allowed the Hebrews to leave, he regretted his decision and changed his mind, ordering his army to bring them back to Egypt. As the people of Israel reached the Sea of Reeds, they saw the Egyptians approaching and were filled with terror. God told Moses to lift his rod and when he did, a strong east wind drove back the sea, leaving space for the Hebrews to cross over on dry land. The Egyptians pursued them, but Moses again lifted his rod and the waters rushed back, drowning the soldiers.

Then Miriam, the sister of Moses, took her timbrel in her hand and all the women followed her in a joyous dance of victory. She led them chanting, "Sing to God who has triumphed gloriously. Horse and rider are hurled into the sea."

Thus, God brought us out of Egypt, not by an angel nor a seraph, nor a messenger, but alone, with a mighty hand and outstretched arm, with great terror and with signs and wonders.

Sunset, Nahariya, Israel, 1995

Maggid Seder Activities

As you tell the Passover story, invite the children to act it out. Use simple costumes and props. Even young children can be involved, since they are not required to speak.

Create a seder trivia game (like Jeopardy or Who Wants to Be A Millionaire?).

Assign each participant a character in the story (e.g. Pharaoh's magician, Shifra the midwife, a soldier, Aaron). Have them take turns being interviewed on a popular "talk show."

Follow a Sephardic custom: Pretend that the youngest child has just left Egypt. Ask where she/he is from and where she/he is going, and what she/he is going to eat and why.

Photocopy the Passover narrative and cut it up into sections. Shuffle the sections and distribute them to willing participants whose job it is to read his or her section at the correct place in the story.

Hold the seder on the floor. (Move the furniture back to the walls or out of the way.) Have each family attending bring a "tribal blanket" to sit on and pillows for reclining.

Invite each person or family attending to bring a poster that tells one thing he/she would like freedom from, freedom for and freedom to. Put up on the walls before the seder begins and discuss during the Maggid section.[17]

Maggid Seder Songs

Let My People Go

(The Biblical story of the Exodus has inspired many people in many places to seek freedom. "Let My People Go "is an African-American spiritual.)

When Israel was in Egypt land,
Let my people go.
Oppressed so hard they could not stand,
Let my people go.

Chorus
Go down Moses, way down in Egypt land.
Tell ol' Pharaoh to let my people go.

"Thus saith the Lord, " bold Moses said.
Let my people go.
"If not I'll smite your first born dead."
Let my people go.

Chorus

Let My People Go, New York City, USA, 1987

Listen, King Pharaoh

Oh listen, Oh listen,
Oh listen King Pharaoh.
Oh listen, Oh listen,
Please let my people go.
They want to go away, they work too hard all day.
King Pharaoh, King Pharaoh, What do you say?
No, no, no! I will not let them go!
No, no, no! I will not let them go!

The Frog Song

(Have the children get up and jump around. If your room is too crowded, have children use handmade puppets, small store bought stuffed animal frogs, or plastic frogs to do the jumping.)

One morning when Pharaoh woke in his bed,
There were frogs on his bed and frogs on his head,
Frogs on his nose and frogs on his toes,
Frogs here, frogs there, frogs were jumping everywhere!

Maggid Commentaries and Questions for Discussion

In Hebrew, "Mitzraim" means a narrow and confined place. Being in "Mitzraim" can be both a physical and spiritual condition. What makes you trapped or stuck in a rut? What helps you leave your "Mitzraim?"

Some scholars say there is no demonstrable historical basis for a Hebrew presence in the land of Egypt; therefore the story is a myth. Others disagree. Does it make a difference to you if you believe the story is historical or mythical?

There is no evidence that the Hebrews would turn against the Pharaoh, yet his irrational fear turns him against them. When have you seen this kind of behavior occur? Why can it be dangerous?

Pharaoh distanced himself emotionally and psychologically from the evil he decreed. For example, he assigned the midwives the task of murdering newborns, and the soldiers the task of tossing babies into the sea. How have modern tyrants designed evil plans for others to enact?

The Torah verse... "And the Egyptians made the Israelites serve with rigor" indicates that ordinary Egyptians were involved in the oppression and were immune to the Israelites suffering. They shared in the guilt and thus were punished.

How can we apply pressure for change? Can there be liberation without violence?

The midwives, Shifra and Puah, performed the world's first recorded act of civil disobedience. Have you, or anyone you know well, been involved with civil disobedience? Share the experience.

Why do you think the Torah tells us the names of the midwives, but omits the name of the reigning Pharaoh? (Most historians agree he was Ramses II.)

The midrash refers to Pharaoh's daughter as "Batya," meaning "daughter of God." This midrash teaches us that the righteous of all people have merit.

Perhaps others passed the burning bush but were not as spiritually open to God's presence in the world as Moses was.[18] What makes people open or closed to spirituality?

In the Torah text, when Moses seeks God's name, God replies, "I Will Be What I Will Be." How would you interpret this name?

What kind of leadership do you think we need today in our country, in Israel, and in the world?

What is the main purpose of the Ten Plagues?
—to punish the Egyptians?
—to display God's might to the Egyptians and to the Hebrews?
—to add drama to the story?

The Torah tells us that "the frog ascended and the land was filled with frogs." The midrash teaches that there is a shift from singular to plural because there was only one frog initially. When the frog saw that no one opposed its move, it whistled for the rest to follow. [19]

We note in the plagues that direct violence against human beings is used as a last resort to achieve political results. How does this apply to our world today?

Before the final plague, the Hebrews were instructed to mark their doorposts with lambs' blood so the angel of death would "pass over" their homes, hence, the name of the holiday.

The rabbis taught that those Hebrews who refused to leave Egypt were not just foolish but wicked. For a Jew to be free is not an opportunity…it is an obligation. Do you agree or disagree? Why do some not find freedom an imperative?

There is a legend that the sea did not split until one person, Nachshon ben Aminadav, had the courage to step in. When were you the first "to step in" like Nachshon and when did you stay on the sidelines?

The Torah says nothing about Miriam's personal life. What do you imagine? Could she have a "career" as a prophet and have a family too?

Even though they left in haste, the women took their timbrels! They were obviously important ceremonial objects. If you were at the Exodus, what would you have been sure to pack?

There is an old Jewish saying, "Pray as if everything depended on God, and act as if everything depended on you." How does this saying relate or not relate to the Passover story?

God's Promise

(The matzot are covered and the wine lifted.)

The Arlen Fern School, Buenos Aires, Argentina, 2002

וְהִיא שֶׁעָמְדָה לַאֲבוֹתֵינוּ וְלָנוּ. שֶׁלֹא אֶחָד בִּלְבָד, עָמַד עָלֵינוּ לְכַלוֹתֵנוּ. אֶלָּא
שֶׁבְּכָל דּוֹר וָדוֹר, עוֹמְדִים עָלֵינוּ לְכַלוֹתֵנוּ. וְהַקָּדוֹשׁ בָּרוּךְ הוּא מַצִּילֵנוּ מִיָּדָם:

*Vehi she'amdah la'avoteinu v'lanu. Shelo echad bilvad, amad aleinu
l'chaloteinu. Ela sheb'chol dor vador, omdim aleinu l'chaloteinu.
VeHakadosh, Baruch Hu, matzileinu miyadam.*

It is the promise of redemption that has sustained the Jewish people in each
generation, as enemies arose who sought to destroy us. And the Holy One of
Blessing saved us from their hand.

Dayenu
(It Would Have Been Sufficient)

How grateful we are for all the different acts of kindness that Adonai has done for us!

Ilu hotzianu miMitzraim . . . . **Dayenu**

Ilu natan lanu et haShabbat . . . . **Dayenu**

Ilu natan lanu et haTorah . . . . **Dayenu**

God. . .

Took us out of Egypt . . . .**Dayenu**

Punished the Egyptians and
destroyed their idols . . . .**Dayenu**

Divided the Sea of Reeds and
led us across on dry land . . . . **Dayenu**

Took care of us in the desert
and fed us manna. . . . .**Dayenu**

Gave us Shabbat. . . . .**Dayenu**

Brought us to Mount Sinai and
gave us the Torah. . . . .**Dayenu**

Brought us to Israel and built
the Temple . . . .**Dayenu**

For all these, we say. . . . .**Dayenu**

כַּמָּה מַעֲלוֹת טוֹבוֹת לַמָּקוֹם עָלֵינוּ:

אִלּוּ הוֹצִיאָנוּ מִמִּצְרַיִם,
וְלֹא עָשָׂה בָהֶם שְׁפָטִים, דַּיֵּנוּ:

אִלּוּ עָשָׂה בָהֶם שְׁפָטִים,
וְלֹא עָשָׂה בֵאלֹהֵיהֶם, דַּיֵּנוּ:

אִלּוּ עָשָׂה בֵאלֹהֵיהֶם,
וְלֹא הָרַג אֶת־בְּכוֹרֵיהֶם, דַּיֵּנוּ:

אִלּוּ הָרַג אֶת־בְּכוֹרֵיהֶם,
וְלֹא נָתַן לָנוּ אֶת־מָמוֹנָם, דַּיֵּנוּ:

אִלּוּ נָתַן לָנוּ אֶת־מָמוֹנָם,
וְלֹא קָרַע לָנוּ אֶת־הַיָּם, דַּיֵּנוּ:

אִלּוּ קָרַע לָנוּ אֶת־הַיָּם,
וְלֹא הֶעֱבִירָנוּ בְתוֹכוֹ בֶּחָרָבָה דַּיֵּנוּ:

אִלּוּ הֶעֱבִירָנוּ בְתוֹכוֹ בֶּחָרָבָה,
וְלֹא שִׁקַּע צָרֵינוּ בְּתוֹכוֹ, דַּיֵּנוּ:

אִלּוּ שִׁקַּע צָרֵינוּ בְּתוֹכוֹ,
וְלֹא סִפֵּק צָרְכֵּנוּ בַּמִּדְבָּר אַרְבָּעִים שָׁנָה, דַּיֵּנוּ:

אִלּוּ סִפֵּק צָרְכֵּנוּ בַּמִּדְבָּר אַרְבָּעִים שָׁנָה,
וְלֹא הֶאֱכִילָנוּ אֶת־הַמָּן, דַּיֵּנוּ:

אִלּוּ הֶאֱכִילָנוּ אֶת־הַמָּן,
וְלֹא נָתַן לָנוּ אֶת־הַשַּׁבָּת, דַּיֵּנוּ:

אִלּוּ נָתַן לָנוּ אֶת־הַשַּׁבָּת,
וְלֹא קֵרְבָנוּ לִפְנֵי הַר סִינַי, דַּיֵּנוּ:

אִלּוּ קֵרְבָנוּ לִפְנֵי הַר סִינַי,
וְלֹא נָתַן לָנוּ אֶת־הַתּוֹרָה, דַּיֵּנוּ:

אִלּוּ נָתַן לָנוּ אֶת־הַתּוֹרָה,
וְלֹא הִכְנִיסָנוּ לְאֶרֶץ יִשְׂרָאֵל, דַּיֵּנוּ:

אִלּוּ הִכְנִיסָנוּ לְאֶרֶץ יִשְׂרָאֵל,
וְלֹא בָנָה לָנוּ אֶת־בֵּית הַבְּחִירָה, דַּיֵּנוּ:

It is an Iranian custom to "whip" each other with scallions during the singing of Dayenu to recall the beatings slaves endured.[20]

The reasons why we praise God grow and grow. We must stop to count each favor. For what other blessings or favors are you grateful?

Dayenu also emphasizes that perfection is not achieved all at once.[21]

Obviously, God was not satisfied until all the steps to our deliverance were achieved.

Mother & Son, Na'it, Yemen, 1993

Oil Pressers, Outside of Alibag, India, 2001

The Passover Symbols

Rabban Gamliel would say, "Those who have not explained three things during the seder have not fulfilled their obligation. These three things are: the Pesach offering, matzah and maror."

Pesach
Our ancestors ate a Passover offering at the time the Temple stood to remember that God passed over the houses of the Hebrews during the tenth plague.

Matzah
The matzah reminds us that our ancestors left Egypt in such great haste that the dough for their bread did not have time to rise.

Maror
Maror reminds us of how bitter the Egyptians made the lives of our ancestors when they were slaves.

Pesach (paschal lamb)

The Hebrews risked their lives slaughtering an animal for the Passover offering that was holy to the Egyptians. In this way, they distanced themselves from paganism and idolatry. From what do we need to distance ourselves today?

The shankbone can also represent the outstretched arms of people in the Passover story: Yocheved, the birth-mother of Moses, as she gently placed her infant son into the basket she wove; Batya, Pharaoh's daughter, as she lifted this newborn into her heart; Miriam, the sister of Moses, as she carried him to Yocheved to nurse; Moses, as he lifted his rod at the Sea of Reeds; and finally, the outstretched arms of the Israelite women as they lifted their timbrels to praise God for deliverance.[22]

The Hebrews ate the paschal lamb with their loins girded, their shoes on, with staff in hand, ready to leave. How can we prepare to be ready to face our own challenges?

The sacrifice of the lamb on Passover was permitted until the destruction of the Temple. Since then, Ashkenazim have been forbidden to eat lamb meat on Passover, but it is the featured dish at the seder meal for some Sephardim.

Matzah

Matzah is called both the bread of poverty and the bread of freedom. Rebbe Nachman of Bratslav taught that the bread itself did not change, its taste did.[23] What did he mean?

Just as our ancestors left for freedom in haste, so we too must move quickly to work for freedom and redemption. What do you think requires our immediate attention?

Maror

Ashkenazim usually use horseradish for maror; Sephardim and Mizrachim (Eastern) Jews use romaine lettuce, escarole or endive lettuce.

Why do you think we recite a blessing upon eating something that is bitter?

Tell about a bitter experience that you or someone you know once had, to which you or they responded in a way that helped others.

עַל אַחַת כַּמָּה וְכַמָּה טוֹבָה כְּפוּלָה וּמְכֻפֶּלֶת לַמָּקוֹם עָלֵינוּ:

שֶׁהוֹצִיאָנוּ מִמִּצְרַיִם,
וְעָשָׂה בָהֶם שְׁפָטִים,
וְעָשָׂה בֵאלֹהֵיהֶם,
וְהָרַג אֶת־בְּכוֹרֵיהֶם,
וְנָתַן לָנוּ אֶת־מָמוֹנָם,
וְקָרַע לָנוּ אֶת־הַיָּם,
וְהֶעֱבִירָנוּ בְתוֹכוֹ בֶּחָרָבָה,
וְשִׁקַּע צָרֵינוּ בְּתוֹכוֹ,
וְסִפֵּק צָרְכֵּנוּ בַּמִּדְבָּר אַרְבָּעִים שָׁנָה,
וְהֶאֱכִילָנוּ אֶת־הַמָּן,
וְנָתַן לָנוּ אֶת־הַשַּׁבָּת,
וְקֵרְבָנוּ לִפְנֵי הַר סִינַי,
וְנָתַן לָנוּ אֶת־הַתּוֹרָה,
וְהִכְנִיסָנוּ לְאֶרֶץ יִשְׂרָאֵל,
וּבָנָה לָנוּ אֶת־בֵּית הַבְּחִירָה,

לְכַפֵּר עַל־כָּל־עֲוֹנוֹתֵינוּ.
רַבָּן גַּמְלִיאֵל הָיָה אוֹמֵר: כָּל שֶׁלֹּא אָמַר שְׁלֹשָׁה דְבָרִים אֵלּוּ בַּפֶּסַח, לֹא יָצָא יְדֵי חוֹבָתוֹ, וְאֵלּוּ הֵן:

פֶּסַח. מַצָּה וּמָרוֹר:

פֶּסַח שֶׁהָיוּ אֲבוֹתֵינוּ אוֹכְלִים, בִּזְמַן שֶׁבֵּית הַמִּקְדָּשׁ הָיָה קַיָּם, עַל שׁוּם מָה? עַל שׁוּם שֶׁפָּסַח הַקָּדוֹשׁ בָּרוּךְ הוּא, עַל בָּתֵּי אֲבוֹתֵינוּ בְּמִצְרַיִם, שֶׁנֶּאֱמַר: וַאֲמַרְתֶּם זֶבַח פֶּסַח הוּא לַיָי, אֲשֶׁר פָּסַח עַל בָּתֵּי בְנֵי יִשְׂרָאֵל בְּמִצְרַיִם, בְּנָגְפּוֹ אֶת־מִצְרַיִם וְאֶת־בָּתֵּינוּ הִצִּיל, וַיִּקֹּד הָעָם וַיִּשְׁתַּחֲוּוּ.

(יגביה המצה ויאמר)
מַצָּה זוֹ שֶׁאָנוּ אוֹכְלִים, עַל שׁוּם

מָה? עַל שׁוּם שֶׁלֹּא הִסְפִּיק בְּצֵקָם שֶׁל אֲבוֹתֵינוּ לְהַחֲמִיץ, עַד שֶׁנִּגְלָה עֲלֵיהֶם מֶלֶךְ מַלְכֵי הַמְּלָכִים, הַקָּדוֹשׁ בָּרוּךְ הוּא, וּגְאָלָם, שֶׁנֶּאֱמַר: וַיֹּאפוּ אֶת־הַבָּצֵק, אֲשֶׁר הוֹצִיאוּ מִמִּצְרַיִם, עֻגֹת מַצּוֹת, כִּי לֹא חָמֵץ: כִּי גֹרְשׁוּ מִמִּצְרַיִם, וְלֹא יָכְלוּ לְהִתְמַהְמֵהַּ, וְגַם צֵדָה לֹא עָשׂוּ לָהֶם.

(יגביה המרור ויאמר)
מָרוֹר זֶה שֶׁאָנוּ אוֹכְלִים, עַל שׁוּם מָה? עַל שׁוּם שֶׁמֵּרְרוּ הַמִּצְרִים אֶת־חַיֵּי אֲבוֹתֵינוּ בְּמִצְרַיִם, שֶׁנֶּאֱמַר: וַיְמָרְרוּ אֶת־חַיֵּיהֶם בַּעֲבֹדָה קָשָׁה, בְּחֹמֶר וּבִלְבֵנִים, וּבְכָל־עֲבֹדָה בַּשָּׂדֶה: אֵת כָּל־עֲבֹדָתָם, אֲשֶׁר עָבְדוּ בָהֶם בְּפָרֶךְ.

Bet Levi Family, Iquitos, Peru, 2003

Holocaust Survivor, Buenos Aires, Argentina, 2002

In Every Generation

בְּכָל־דּוֹר וָדוֹר חַיָּב אָדָם לִרְאוֹת אֶת־עַצְמוֹ, כְּאִלּוּ הוּא יָצָא מִמִּצְרָיִם.

B'chol dor vador, chayav adam lirot et atzmo k'ilu hu yatza miMitzraim.

In every generation, each person must view himself or herself as having personally gone out of Egypt.

How can we, who have never been enslaved nor witnessed such deliverance, feel as if we were there?

How can those who were, or those who are now not physically free, participate in a seder that proclaims God's redemption?

Although we each have this responsibility as individuals, why do we tell the story together?

The phrase "in every generation" implies that we must relate the story of the Exodus to our particular circumstances. How would you say it applies today?

As you look at the photographs in this Haggadah, you can imagine being Jewish in different parts of the world. Ask each participant to select a favorite one and talk about it as if he or she were the subject of the photograph.

Klezmer Duo, Buenos Aires, Argentina, 2002

שֶׁנֶּאֱמַר: וְהִגַּדְתָּ לְבִנְךָ בַּיּוֹם הַהוּא לֵאמֹר: בַּעֲבוּר זֶה עָשָׂה יְיָ לִי, בְּצֵאתִי מִמִּצְרָיִם. לֹא אֶת־אֲבוֹתֵינוּ בִּלְבָד, גָּאַל הַקָּדוֹשׁ בָּרוּךְ הוּא, אֶלָּא אַף אוֹתָנוּ גָּאַל עִמָּהֶם, שֶׁנֶּאֱמַר:

(יגביה הכוס, יכסה המצות ויאמר)

וְאוֹתָנוּ הוֹצִיא מִשָּׁם, לְמַעַן הָבִיא אֹתָנוּ, לָתֶת לָנוּ אֶת־הָאָרֶץ אֲשֶׁר נִשְׁבַּע לַאֲבֹתֵינוּ.

לְפִיכָךְ אֲנַחְנוּ חַיָּבִים לְהוֹדוֹת, לְהַלֵּל, לְשַׁבֵּחַ, לְפָאֵר, לְרוֹמֵם,

לְהַדֵּר, לְבָרֵךְ, לְעַלֵּה וּלְקַלֵּס, לְמִי שֶׁעָשָׂה לַאֲבוֹתֵינוּ וְלָנוּ אֶת־כָּל־הַנִּסִּים הָאֵלּוּ. הוֹצִיאָנוּ מֵעַבְדוּת לְחֵרוּת, מִיָּגוֹן לְשִׂמְחָה, וּמֵאֵבֶל לְיוֹם טוֹב, וּמֵאֲפֵלָה לְאוֹר גָּדוֹל, וּמִשִּׁעְבּוּד לִגְאֻלָּה.

Songs of Praise

(Lift the wine cups and recite.)

Therefore, it is our duty to thank, to praise, to laud, to glorify, to exalt, to honor, to bless, to elevate and to extol the One who performed all these miracles for our ancestors and for us.

God took us from slavery to freedom, from sadness to joy, from mourning to celebration, from darkness to light, and from subjugation to redemption.

וְנֹאמַר לְפָנָיו שִׁירָה חֲדָשָׁה. הַלְלוּיָהּ.

V'nomar l'fanav shira chadasha, Halleluyah.

Therefore let us sing a new song, Halleluyah.

הַלְלוּיָהּ. הַלְלוּ עַבְדֵי יְיָ. הַלְלוּ אֶת־שֵׁם יְיָ. יְהִי שֵׁם יְיָ מְבֹרָךְ מֵעַתָּה וְעַד עוֹלָם:

Halleluyah (2x) hallelu avdei Adonai	הַלְלוּיָהּ. הַלְלוּ עַבְדֵי יְיָ.
Halleluyah (2x) hallelu et shem Adonai	הַלְלוּיָהּ. הַלְלוּ אֶת־שֵׁם יְיָ.
Yehi shem Adonai m'vorach	יְהִי שֵׁם יְיָ מְבֹרָךְ
Me'atah v'ad olam. (Repeat last two lines.)	מֵעַתָּה וְעַד עוֹלָם:
Halleluyah	הַלְלוּיָהּ.

Give praise to Adonai.
Sing praises those who serve Adonai. Blessed is the name of Adonai now and forever.

[Traditional Text]

הַלְלוּיָהּ.הַלְלוּ עַבְדֵי יְיָ. הַלְלוּ אֶת־שֵׁם יְיָ. יְהִי שֵׁם יְיָ מְבֹרָךְ מֵעַתָּה וְעַד עוֹלָם: מִמִּזְרַח שֶׁמֶשׁ עַד מְבוֹאוֹ. מְהֻלָּל שֵׁם יְיָ. רָם עַל־כָּל־גּוֹיִם יְיָ. עַל הַשָּׁמַיִם כְּבוֹדוֹ: מִי כַּיְיָ אֱלֹהֵינוּ. הַמַּגְבִּיהִי לָשָׁבֶת: הַמַּשְׁפִּילִי לִרְאוֹת בַּשָּׁמַיִם וּבָאָרֶץ: מְקִימִי מֵעָפָר דָּל. מֵאַשְׁפֹּת יָרִים אֶבְיוֹן: לְהוֹשִׁיבִי עִם־נְדִיבִים. עִם נְדִיבֵי עַמּוֹ: מוֹשִׁיבִי עֲקֶרֶת הַבַּיִת אֵם הַבָּנִים שְׂמֵחָה. הַלְלוּיָהּ:

B'tzeit Yisrael miMitrayim	בְּצֵאת יִשְׂרָאֵל מִמִּצְרָיִם,
Bet Yaakov me'am lo'ez.	בֵּית יַעֲקֹב מֵעַם לֹעֵז:
Hay'tah Yehudah l'kadsho;	הָיְתָה יְהוּדָה לְקָדְשׁוֹ,
Yisrael mamsh'lotav.	יִשְׂרָאֵל מַמְשְׁלוֹתָיו:
Hayam ra'ah vayanos;	הַיָּם רָאָה וַיָּנֹס,
Hayarden yisov l'achor.	הַיַּרְדֵּן יִסֹּב לְאָחוֹר:
Heharim rak'du ch'eilim;	הֶהָרִים רָקְדוּ כְאֵילִים,
G'vaot kivnei tzon.	גְּבָעוֹת כִּבְנֵי־צֹאן:
Mah l'cha hayam ki tanus;	מַה־לְּךָ הַיָּם כִּי תָנוּס,
HaYarden tisov l'achor.	הַיַּרְדֵּן תִּסֹּב לְאָחוֹר:
Heharim tirk'du ch'eilim;	הֶהָרִים תִּרְקְדוּ כְאֵילִים,
G'vaot kivnei tzon.	גְּבָעוֹת כִּבְנֵי־צֹאן:
Milifnei adon chuli aretz;	מִלִּפְנֵי אָדוֹן חוּלִי אָרֶץ,
Milifnei Elohai Ya'akov.	מִלִּפְנֵי אֱלוֹהַ יַעֲקֹב:
Hahofchi hatzur agam mayim;	הַהֹפְכִי הַצּוּר אֲגַם־מָיִם,
Chalamish l'maino mayim.	חַלָּמִישׁ לְמַעְיְנוֹ־מָיִם:

When Israel left Egypt, when the House of Jacob left these foreign people, Judah became God's holy one, Israel God's dominion. The sea fled at the sight, the Jordan River retreated. The mountains skipped like rams, the hills like lambs, before the presence of the Creator who turns rock into pools of water and flint into fountains.

(Lift the wine cups and recite.)

Blessed are You Adonai, Sovereign of the world, who has redeemed our ancestors and us from Egypt and brought us here this night to eat matzah and maror. Adonai our God, and God of our ancestors, enable us to celebrate future holidays and festivals in peace and in joy. Then we will praise You with a new song.

Baruch Atah Adonai, Ga'al Yisrael.

בָּרוּךְ אַתָּה יְיָ, אֱלֹהֵינוּ מֶלֶךְ הָעוֹלָם, אֲשֶׁר גְּאָלָנוּ וְגָאַל אֶת־אֲבוֹתֵינוּ מִמִּצְרַיִם, וְהִגִּיעָנוּ לַלַּיְלָה הַזֶּה, לֶאֱכָל־בּוֹ מַצָּה וּמָרוֹר. כֵּן, יְיָ אֱלֹהֵינוּ וֵאלֹהֵי אֲבוֹתֵינוּ, יַגִּיעֵנוּ לְמוֹעֲדִים וְלִרְגָלִים אֲחֵרִים, הַבָּאִים לִקְרָאתֵנוּ לְשָׁלוֹם. שְׂמֵחִים בְּבִנְיַן עִירֶךָ, וְשָׂשִׂים בַּעֲבוֹדָתֶךָ, וְנֹאכַל שָׁם מִן הַזְּבָחִים וּמִן הַפְּסָחִים (במוצאי שבת יש אומרים: מִן הַפְּסָחִים וּמִן הַזְּבָחִים), אֲשֶׁר יַגִּיעַ דָּמָם, עַל קִיר מִזְבַּחֲךָ לְרָצוֹן, וְנוֹדֶה לְךָ שִׁיר חָדָשׁ עַל גְּאֻלָּתֵנוּ, וְעַל פְּדוּת נַפְשֵׁנוּ:בָּרוּךְ אַתָּה יְיָ, גָּאַל יִשְׂרָאֵל:

Blessed are You, Adonai our God, redeemer of the people Israel.

Second Cup – "I Will Rescue You."

We are now ready for the second cup of wine, which we drink while reclining.

בָּרוּךְ אַתָּה יְיָ, אֱלֹהֵינוּ מֶלֶךְ הָעוֹלָם, בּוֹרֵא פְּרִי הַגָּפֶן.

Baruch Atah Adonai, Eloheinu melech haolam, borei p'ree hagafen.

Blessed are You Adonai, Sovereign of the world, who creates the fruit of the vine.

(Drink the second cup while reclining.)

Reflection, The Jordan River, Israel, 2002

Amiaz Plains, Israel 2002

WE WASH OUR HANDS
AND SAY A BLESSING

We wash our hands for the meal and recite the blessing:

בָּרוּךְ אַתָּה יְיָ אֱלֹהֵינוּ מֶלֶךְ הָעוֹלָם, אֲשֶׁר קִדְּשָׁנוּ בְּמִצְוֹתָיו,
וְצִוָּנוּ עַל נְטִילַת יָדָיִם:

Baruch Atah Adonai, Eloheinu melech haolam, asher kid'shanu b'mitzvotav,
v'tzivanu al n'tilat yadayim.

Blessed are You, Adonai our God, Sovereign of the world, who has made us holy through
Your mitzvot, and commanded us to wash our hands.

WE SAY THE BLESSING
FOR "BREAD" AND MATZAH

(Distribute pieces of the upper and middle matzah.)

We recite the two blessings for "bread" and matzah:

בָּרוּךְ אַתָּה יְיָ, אֱלֹהֵינוּ מֶלֶךְ הָעוֹלָם, הַמוֹצִיא לֶחֶם מִן הָאָרֶץ:

Baruch Atah Adonai, Eloheinu melech haolam, hamotzi lechem min ha'aretz.

Blessed are You, Adonai our God, Sovereign of the world, who brings forth bread from the earth.

בָּרוּךְ אַתָּה יְיָ, אֱלֹהֵינוּ מֶלֶךְ הָעוֹלָם, אֲשֶׁר קִדְּשָׁנוּ בְּמִצְוֹתָיו
וְצִוָּנוּ עַל אֲכִילַת מַצָּה:

Baruch Atah Adonai, Eloheinu melech haolam, asher kid'shanu b'mitzvotav, v'tzivanu al achilat matzah.

Blessed are You, Adonai our God, Sovereign of the world, who made us holy by Your mitzvot and commanded us to eat matzah.

(Eat the matzah.)

DIP THE BITTER HERB

(Give everyone a piece of maror and some charoset.)

We now dip the maror into the charoset to recall how the bitterness of slavery was withstood because it was sweetened by faith.

בָּרוּךְ אַתָּה יְיָ אֱלֹהֵינוּ מֶלֶךְ הָעוֹלָם, אֲשֶׁר קִדְּשָׁנוּ בְּמִצְוֹתָיו וְצִוָּנוּ עַל אֲכִילַת מָרוֹר:

Baruch Atah Adonai, Eloheinu melech haolam, asher kid'shanu b'mitzvotav, v'tzivanu al achilat maror.

Blessed are You, Adonai our God, Sovereign of the world, who made us holy by Your mitzvot, and commanded us to eat maror.

EAT A SANDWICH WITH MATZAH AND MAROR

(Distribute pieces of maror and pieces of the bottom matzah.)

We do as the sage Hillel did in Temple times. He would make a sandwich of the Pesach (lamb offering) with the matzah and maror. Since we no longer bring sacrifices, our sandwich only has matzah and maror.

(Eat the Hillel sandwich.)

זֵכֶר לְמִקְדָּשׁ כְּהִלֵּל: כֵּן עָשָׂה הִלֵּל בִּזְמַן שֶׁבֵּית הַמִּקְדָּשׁ הָיָה
קַיָם. הָיָה כּוֹרֵךְ פֶּסַח מַצָּה וּמָרוֹר וְאוֹכֵל בְּיַחַד. לְקַיֵם מַה
שֶׁנֶּאֱמַר: עַל־מַצּוֹת וּמְרוֹרִים יֹאכְלֻהוּ:

Hillel lived in Jerusalem during the first century B.C.E. where he founded a school that was known as the "House of Hillel." It was a major influence in the development of rabbinic Judaism. He was known for his patience.

Once, a pagan asked Hillel to teach him the Torah while he stood on one foot. Hillel answered kindly, "That which is hateful to you, do not do to your neighbor. That is the whole Torah. All the rest is commentary; now go and learn."

If you were asked to explain Judaism while someone stood on one foot, what would you say?

שֻׁלְחָן עוֹרֵךְ

WE EAT THE MEAL

New Immigrant, Lod, Israel, 1997

In many homes, hardboiled eggs are served to start the meal as a symbol of fertility and the circle of life. Some add that this act honors the midwives, Shifra and Puah, who saved the lives of Jewish male babies. A third interpretation is that like an egg that gets harder the more it is cooked, the Hebrew's resistance grew tougher the more they were oppressed.

The roasted egg on the seder plate represents the sacrifice that was brought to the Temple on each of the Pilgrimage Festivals.

In Sephardic homes, the roasted egg is eaten at the conclusion of the meal by the firstborn son in gratitude for being spared during the tenth plague.[24]

A new custom is to pass around a dish of olives to eat as a symbol of our hope for peace.

WE EAT THE AFIKOMEN

After the Afikomen is found or ransomed, it is shared with all participants, as the Pesach offering was shared in the time of the Temple. No special blessing is said because the Afikomen, the dessert matzah, is part of the meal. We eat it reclining and without delay. We are not allowed to eat anything after the Afikomen, since its taste must linger in our mouths.

In many Sephardic homes, it is customary to wrap the Afikomen in a sock and for each participant to sling it over his/her shoulder to symbolize leaving Egypt.[25]

The word "Afikomen" is derived from the Greek word "epicumen" which means a food eaten for pleasure, or a dessert. The Afikomen should leave us with a lingering taste that captures all we have derived from the meal. Do you think matzah was a good choice for the Afikomen?

After the meal, we taste a piece of the Afikomen, (the larger piece of the middle matzah) to affirm our belief that completeness will come in the future, according to God's promise.

Why do we hide the Afikomen?
—So no one will eat it before it is time to be used as the "dessert" of the seder meal.
—To symbolically destroy the evil hidden inside our hearts.
—To keep the children's attention as long as possible.

In some homes, the leader hides the Afikomen and the children search for it to receive a reward. In other homes, the children hide it and return it for a "ransom." A fun idea is to give the children clues via a "Twenty Questions" game. This not only provides another opportunity for questions, but also fosters cooperation rather than competition, as the children work together to narrow down the location.[26]

Grace after a Meal, Casablanca, Morocco, 2004

WE SAY THE BLESSING AFTER THE MEAL

(Pour the third cup of wine.)

(This is an abbreviated version of the Blessing After Meals.)

בָּרוּךְ אַתָּה יְיָ, אֱלֹהֵינוּ מֶלֶךְ הָעוֹלָם, הַזָּן אֶת הָעוֹלָם כֻּלּוֹ בְּטוּבוֹ בְּחֵן בְּחֶסֶד וּבְרַחֲמִים הוּא נוֹתֵן לֶחֶם לְכָל בָּשָׂר כִּי לְעוֹלָם חַסְדּוֹ. וּבְטוּבוֹ הַגָּדוֹל תָּמִיד לֹא חָסַר לָנוּ, וְאַל יֶחְסַר לָנוּ מָזוֹן לְעוֹלָם וָעֶד. בַּעֲבוּר שְׁמוֹ הַגָּדוֹל, כִּי הוּא אֵל זָן וּמְפַרְנֵס לַכֹּל וּמֵטִיב לַכֹּל, וּמֵכִין מָזוֹן לְכָל בְּרִיּוֹתָיו אֲשֶׁר בָּרָא. בָּרוּךְ אַתָּה יְיָ, הַזָּן אֶת הַכֹּל.

עֹשֶׂה שָׁלוֹם בִּמְרוֹמָיו, הוּא יַעֲשֶׂה שָׁלוֹם, עָלֵינוּ וְעַל כָּל יִשְׂרָאֵל, וְאִמְרוּ אָמֵן.

Baruch Atah Adonai Eloheinu melech ha'olam, hazan et ha'olam kulo b'tuvo b'chen b'chesed uv'rachamin. Hu noten lechem l'chol basar ki l'olam chasdo. Uv'tuvo hagadol tamid lo chasar lanu v'al yech'sar lanu mazon l'olam va'ed. Ba'avur sh'mo hagadol ki hu zan um'farnes lakol umetiv lakol umechin mazon l'chol b'riyotav asher bara. Baruch Atah Adonai hazan et hakol.

Blessed are You, Adonai our God, Sovereign of the world, who in goodness, mercy and kindness gives food to the world. Your love for us endures forever. We praise You Adonai, who provides sustenance for all life.

May the One who makes peace in the heavens, make peace for us, for Israel, and for all humanity.

(On the next two pages is a complete Birkat HaMazon.)

שִׁיר הַמַּעֲלוֹת בְּשׁוּב יְיָ אֶת שִׁיבַת צִיּוֹן הָיִינוּ כְּחֹלְמִים: אָז יִמָּלֵא שְׂחוֹק פִּינוּ וּלְשׁוֹנֵנוּ רִנָּה אָז יֹאמְרוּ בַגּוֹיִם הִגְדִּיל יְיָ לַעֲשׂוֹת עִם אֵלֶּה: הִגְדִּיל יְיָ לַעֲשׂוֹת עִמָּנוּ הָיִינוּ שְׂמֵחִים: שׁוּבָה יְיָ אֶת שְׁבִיתֵנוּ כַּאֲפִיקִים בַּנֶּגֶב: הַזֹּרְעִים בְּדִמְעָה בְּרִנָּה יִקְצֹרוּ: הָלוֹךְ יֵלֵךְ וּבָכֹה נֹשֵׂא מֶשֶׁךְ הַזָּרַע בֹּא יָבֹא בְרִנָּה נֹשֵׂא אֲלֻמֹּתָיו:

רַבּוֹתַי נְבָרֵךְ!
יְהִי שֵׁם יְיָ מְבֹרָךְ מֵעַתָּה וְעַד עוֹלָם.
יְהִי שֵׁם יְיָ מְבֹרָךְ מֵעַתָּה וְעַד עוֹלָם. בִּרְשׁוּת מָרָנָן וְרַבָּנָן וְרַבּוֹתַי, נְבָרֵךְ (אֱלֹהֵינוּ) שֶׁאָכַלְנוּ מִשֶּׁלּוֹ.
בָּרוּךְ (אֱלֹהֵינוּ) שֶׁאָכַלְנוּ מִשֶּׁלּוֹ וּבְטוּבוֹ חָיִינוּ.
בָּרוּךְ (אֱלֹהֵינוּ) שֶׁאָכַלְנוּ מִשֶּׁלּוֹ וּבְטוּבוֹ חָיִינוּ.

בָּרוּךְ הוּא וּבָרוּךְ שְׁמוֹ:
בָּרוּךְ אַתָּה יְיָ, אֱלֹהֵינוּ מֶלֶךְ הָעוֹלָם, הַזָּן אֶת הָעוֹלָם כֻּלּוֹ בְּטוּבוֹ בְּחֵן בְּחֶסֶד וּבְרַחֲמִים הוּא נוֹתֵן לֶחֶם לְכָל בָּשָׂר כִּי לְעוֹלָם חַסְדּוֹ. וּבְטוּבוֹ הַגָּדוֹל תָּמִיד לֹא חָסַר לָנוּ, וְאַל יֶחְסַר לָנוּ מָזוֹן לְעוֹלָם וָעֶד. בַּעֲבוּר שְׁמוֹ הַגָּדוֹל, כִּי הוּא אֵל זָן וּמְפַרְנֵס לַכֹּל וּמֵטִיב לַכֹּל, וּמֵכִין מָזוֹן לְכָל בְּרִיּוֹתָיו אֲשֶׁר בָּרָא. בָּרוּךְ אַתָּה יְיָ, הַזָּן אֶת הַכֹּל:

נוֹדֶה לְּךָ יְיָ אֱלֹהֵינוּ עַל שֶׁהִנְחַלְתָּ לַאֲבוֹתֵינוּ, אֶרֶץ חֶמְדָּה טוֹבָה וּרְחָבָה, וְעַל שֶׁהוֹצֵאתָנוּ יְיָ אֱלֹהֵינוּ מֵאֶרֶץ מִצְרַיִם, וּפְדִיתָנוּ, מִבֵּית עֲבָדִים, וְעַל בְּרִיתְךָ שֶׁחָתַמְתָּ בִּבְשָׂרֵנוּ, וְעַל תּוֹרָתְךָ שֶׁלִּמַּדְתָּנוּ, וְעַל חֻקֶּיךָ שֶׁהוֹדַעְתָּנוּ וְעַל חַיִּים חֵן וָחֶסֶד שֶׁחוֹנַנְתָּנוּ, וְעַל אֲכִילַת מָזוֹן שָׁאַתָּה זָן וּמְפַרְנֵס אוֹתָנוּ תָּמִיד, בְּכָל יוֹם וּבְכָל עֵת וּבְכָל שָׁעָה:

וְעַל הַכֹּל יְיָ אֱלֹהֵינוּ אֲנַחְנוּ מוֹדִים לָךְ, וּמְבָרְכִים אוֹתָךְ, יִתְבָּרַךְ שִׁמְךָ בְּפִי כָּל חַי תָּמִיד לְעוֹלָם וָעֶד. כַּכָּתוּב, וְאָכַלְתָּ וְשָׂבָעְתָּ, וּבֵרַכְתָּ אֶת יְיָ אֱלֹהֶיךָ עַל הָאָרֶץ הַטֹּבָה אֲשֶׁר נָתַן לָךְ. בָּרוּךְ אַתָּה יְיָ, עַל הָאָרֶץ וְעַל הַמָּזוֹן:

רַחֶם נָא יְיָ אֱלֹהֵינוּ, עַל יִשְׂרָאֵל עַמֶּךָ, וְעַל יְרוּשָׁלַיִם עִירֶךָ, וְעַל צִיּוֹן מִשְׁכַּן כְּבוֹדֶךָ, וְעַל מַלְכוּת בֵּית דָּוִד מְשִׁיחֶךָ, וְעַל הַבַּיִת הַגָּדוֹל וְהַקָּדוֹשׁ שֶׁנִּקְרָא שִׁמְךָ עָלָיו. אֱלֹהֵינוּ, אָבִינוּ, רְעֵנוּ, זוּנֵנוּ, פַּרְנְסֵנוּ, וְכַלְכְּלֵנוּ, וְהַרְוִיחֵנוּ, וְהַרְוַח לָנוּ יְיָ אֱלֹהֵינוּ מְהֵרָה מִכָּל צָרוֹתֵינוּ, וְנָא, אַל תַּצְרִיכֵנוּ יְיָ אֱלֹהֵינוּ, לֹא לִידֵי מַתְּנַת בָּשָׂר וָדָם, וְלֹא לִידֵי הַלְוָאָתָם. כִּי אִם לְיָדְךָ הַמְּלֵאָה, הַפְּתוּחָה, הַקְּדוֹשָׁה וְהָרְחָבָה, שֶׁלֹּא נֵבוֹשׁ וְלֹא נִכָּלֵם לְעוֹלָם וָעֶד:

לשבת רְצֵה וְהַחֲלִיצֵנוּ יְיָ אֱלֹהֵינוּ בְּמִצְוֹתֶיךָ וּבְמִצְוַת יוֹם הַשְּׁבִיעִי הַשַּׁבָּת הַגָּדוֹל וְהַקָּדוֹשׁ הַזֶּה. כִּי יוֹם זֶה גָּדוֹל וְקָדוֹשׁ הוּא לְפָנֶיךָ, לִשְׁבָּת בּוֹ וְלָנוּחַ בּוֹ בְּאַהֲבָה כְּמִצְוַת רְצוֹנֶךָ וּבִרְצוֹנְךָ הָנִיחַ לָנוּ יְיָ אֱלֹהֵינוּ, שֶׁלֹּא תְהֵא צָרָה וְיָגוֹן וַאֲנָחָה בְּיוֹם מְנוּחָתֵנוּ. וְהַרְאֵנוּ יְיָ אֱלֹהֵינוּ בְּנֶחָמַת צִיּוֹן עִירֶךָ, וּבְבִנְיַן יְרוּשָׁלַיִם עִיר קָדְשֶׁךָ, כִּי אַתָּה הוּא בַּעַל הַיְשׁוּעוֹת וּבַעַל הַנֶּחָמוֹת:

אֱלֹהֵינוּ וֵאלֹהֵי אֲבוֹתֵינוּ, יַעֲלֶה וְיָבֹא וְיַגִּיעַ, וְיֵרָאֶה, וְיֵרָצֶה, וְיִשָּׁמַע, וְיִפָּקֵד, וְיִזָּכֵר זִכְרוֹנֵנוּ וּפִקְדוֹנֵנוּ, וְזִכְרוֹן אֲבוֹתֵינוּ, וְזִכְרוֹן מָשִׁיחַ בֶּן דָּוִד עַבְדֶּךָ, וְזִכְרוֹן יְרוּשָׁלַיִם עִיר קָדְשֶׁךָ, וְזִכְרוֹן כָּל עַמְּךָ בֵּית יִשְׂרָאֵל לְפָנֶיךָ, לִפְלֵיטָה לְטוֹבָה לְחֵן וּלְחֶסֶד וּלְרַחֲמִים, לְחַיִּים וּלְשָׁלוֹם בְּיוֹם חַג הַמַּצּוֹת הַזֶּה. זָכְרֵנוּ יְיָ אֱלֹהֵינוּ בּוֹ לְטוֹבָה. וּפָקְדֵנוּ בוֹ לִבְרָכָה. וְהוֹשִׁיעֵנוּ בוֹ לְחַיִּים, וּבִדְבַר יְשׁוּעָה וְרַחֲמִים, חוּס וְחָנֵּנוּ, וְרַחֵם עָלֵינוּ וְהוֹשִׁיעֵנוּ, כִּי אֵלֶיךָ עֵינֵינוּ, כִּי אֵל מֶלֶךְ חַנּוּן וְרַחוּם אָתָּה:

וּבְנֵה יְרוּשָׁלַיִם עִיר הַקֹּדֶשׁ בִּמְהֵרָה בְיָמֵינוּ. בָּרוּךְ אַתָּה יְיָ, בּוֹנֵה בְרַחֲמָיו יְרוּשָׁלַיִם. אָמֵן

בָּרוּךְ אַתָּה יְיָ אֱלֹהֵינוּ מֶלֶךְ הָעוֹלָם, הָאֵל אָבִינוּ, מַלְכֵּנוּ, אַדִירֵנוּ בּוֹרְאֵנוּ, גּוֹאֲלֵנוּ, יוֹצְרֵנוּ, קְדוֹשֵׁנוּ קְדוֹשׁ יַעֲקֹב, רוֹעֵנוּ רוֹעֵה יִשְׂרָאֵל, הַמֶּלֶךְ הַטּוֹב, וְהַמֵּטִיב לַכֹּל, שֶׁבְּכָל יוֹם וָיוֹם הוּא הֵטִיב, הוּא מֵטִיב, הוּא יֵיטִיב לָנוּ. הוּא גְמָלָנוּ, הוּא גוֹמְלֵנוּ, הוּא יִגְמְלֵנוּ לָעַד לְחֵן וּלְחֶסֶד וּלְרַחֲמִים וּלְרֶוַח הַצָּלָה וְהַצְלָחָה בְּרָכָה וִישׁוּעָה, נֶחָמָה, פַּרְנָסָה וְכַלְכָּלָה, וְרַחֲמִים, וְחַיִּים וְשָׁלוֹם, וְכָל טוֹב, וּמִכָּל טוֹב לְעוֹלָם אַל יְחַסְּרֵנוּ:

הָרַחֲמָן, הוּא יִמְלוֹךְ עָלֵינוּ לְעוֹלָם וָעֶד.

הָרַחֲמָן, הוּא יִתְבָּרַךְ בַּשָּׁמַיִם וּבָאָרֶץ.

הָרַחֲמָן, הוּא יִשְׁתַּבַּח לְדוֹר דּוֹרִים, וְיִתְפָּאַר בָּנוּ לָעַד וּלְנֵצַח נְצָחִים, וְיִתְהַדַּר בָּנוּ לָעַד וּלְעוֹלְמֵי עוֹלָמִים.

הָרַחֲמָן, הוּא יְפַרְנְסֵנוּ בְּכָבוֹד.

הָרַחֲמָן, הוּא יִשְׁבּוֹר עֻלֵּנוּ מֵעַל צַוָּארֵנוּ וְהוּא יוֹלִיכֵנוּ קוֹמְמִיּוּת לְאַרְצֵנוּ.

הָרַחֲמָן, הוּא יִשְׁלַח לָנוּ בְּרָכָה מְרֻבָּה בַּבַּיִת הַזֶּה, וְעַל שֻׁלְחָן זֶה שֶׁאָכַלְנוּ עָלָיו.

הָרַחֲמָן, הוּא יִשְׁלַח לָנוּ אֶת אֵלִיָּהוּ הַנָּבִיא זָכוּר לַטּוֹב, וִיבַשֶּׂר לָנוּ בְּשׂוֹרוֹת טוֹבוֹת יְשׁוּעוֹת וְנֶחָמוֹת.

הָרַחֲמָן, הוּא יְבָרֵךְ אֶת (אָבִי מוֹרִי) בַּעַל הַבַּיִת הַזֶּה, וְאֶת (אִמִּי מוֹרָתִי) בַּעֲלַת הַבַּיִת הַזֶּה,

הָרַחֲמָן, הוּא יְבָרֵךְ אוֹתִי (וְאָבִי וְאִמִּי וְאִשְׁתִּי וְזַרְעִי וְאֶת כָּל אֲשֶׁר לִי)

הָרַחֲמָן, הוּא יְבָרֵךְ אֶת בַּעַל הַבַּיִת הַזֶּה, וְאֶת אִשְׁתּוֹ בַּעֲלַת הַבַּיִת הַזֶּה.

אוֹתָם וְאֶת בֵּיתָם וְאֶת זַרְעָם וְאֶת כָּל אֲשֶׁר לָהֶם אוֹתָנוּ וְאֶת כָּל אֲשֶׁר לָנוּ, כְּמוֹ שֶׁנִּתְבָּרְכוּ אֲבוֹתֵינוּ, אַבְרָהָם יִצְחָק וְיַעֲקֹב: בַּכֹּל, מִכֹּל, כֹּל. כֵּן יְבָרֵךְ אוֹתָנוּ כֻּלָּנוּ יַחַד. בִּבְרָכָה שְׁלֵמָה, וְנֹאמַר אָמֵן:

בַּמָּרוֹם יְלַמְּדוּ עֲלֵיהֶם וְעָלֵינוּ זְכוּת, שֶׁתְּהֵא לְמִשְׁמֶרֶת שָׁלוֹם, וְנִשָּׂא בְרָכָה מֵאֵת יְיָ וּצְדָקָה מֵאֱלֹהֵי יִשְׁעֵנוּ, וְנִמְצָא חֵן וְשֵׂכֶל טוֹב בְּעֵינֵי אֱלֹהִים וְאָדָם:

לשבת הָרַחֲמָן, הוּא יַנְחִילֵנוּ יוֹם שֶׁכֻּלּוֹ שַׁבָּת וּמְנוּחָה לְחַיֵּי הָעוֹלָמִים.

הָרַחֲמָן, הוּא יַנְחִילֵנוּ יוֹם שֶׁכֻּלּוֹ טוֹב.

הָרַחֲמָן, הוּא יְזַכֵּנוּ לִימוֹת הַמָּשִׁיחַ וּלְחַיֵּי הָעוֹלָם הַבָּא. מִגְדּוֹל יְשׁוּעוֹת מַלְכּוֹ, וְעֹשֶׂה חֶסֶד לִמְשִׁיחוֹ לְדָוִד וּלְזַרְעוֹ עַד עוֹלָם: עֹשֶׂה שָׁלוֹם בִּמְרוֹמָיו, הוּא יַעֲשֶׂה שָׁלוֹם, עָלֵינוּ וְעַל כָּל יִשְׂרָאֵל, וְאִמְרוּ אָמֵן:

יְראוּ אֶת יְיָ קְדֹשָׁיו, כִּי אֵין מַחְסוֹר לִירֵאָיו: כְּפִירִים רָשׁוּ וְרָעֵבוּ, וְדֹרְשֵׁי יְיָ לֹא יַחְסְרוּ כָל טוֹב: הוֹדוּ לַיְיָ כִּי טוֹב, כִּי לְעוֹלָם חַסְדּוֹ: פּוֹתֵחַ אֶת יָדֶךָ, וּמַשְׂבִּיעַ לְכָל חַי רָצוֹן: בָּרוּךְ הַגֶּבֶר אֲשֶׁר יִבְטַח בַּיְיָ, וְהָיָה יְיָ מִבְטַחוֹ: נַעַר הָיִיתִי גַם זָקַנְתִּי וְלֹא רָאִיתִי צַדִּיק נֶעֱזָב, וְזַרְעוֹ מְבַקֶּשׁ לָחֶם: יְיָ עֹז לְעַמּוֹ יִתֵּן, יְיָ יְבָרֵךְ אֶת עַמּוֹ בַשָּׁלוֹם:

The Third Cup – " I Will Redeem You."

(Lift the wine cups.)

We are now ready for the third cup of wine, which we drink while reclining.

בָּרוּךְ אַתָּה יְיָ, אֱלֹהֵינוּ מֶלֶךְ הָעוֹלָם, בּוֹרֵא פְּרִי הַגָּפֶן:

Baruch Atah Adonai, Eloheinu melech haolam, borai p'ree hagafen.

Blessed are You, Adonai our God, Sovereign of the world, who creates the fruit of the vine.

(Drink the third cup while reclining.)

Pour Out Your Wrath

(Some open the door at this point and close it after the recitation.)

We express our anxieties and trepidation about those now involved in evil. We ask God to deal with them accordingly and hope we ourselves will be spared confrontation.

שְׁפֹךְ חֲמָתְךָ אֶל־הַגּוֹיִם, אֲשֶׁר לֹא יְדָעוּךָ וְעַל־מַמְלָכוֹת אֲשֶׁר בְּשִׁמְךָ לֹא קָרָאוּ: כִּי אָכַל אֶת־יַעֲקֹב. וְאֶת־נָוֵהוּ הֵשַׁמּוּ: שְׁפָךְ־עֲלֵיהֶם זַעְמֶךָ, וַחֲרוֹן אַפְּךָ יַשִּׂיגֵם: תִּרְדֹּף בְּאַף וְתַשְׁמִידֵם, מִתַּחַת שְׁמֵי יְיָ:

Pour out Your wrath on the nations that do not recognize You or do not invoke Your name. For they have destroyed Jacob and his habitation. (Some Sephardic texts stop here.) Pour forth Your indignation and let your burning anger overtake the wicked. Pursue them and obliterate them.

When should we give up our anger and when should we not?

There is a Talmudic tale about how once Rabbi Meir prayed for the death of two troublesome thieves in the community. His wife, the learned Bruria, urged him to pray instead for the removal of wickedness. He did, and the thieves repented.

Folk Singer, Aspen, Colorado, USA, 1996

Welcoming Miriam

(Pour a cup of water and put it in the center of the table.)

We drink from the prophet Miriam's cup to symbolize the sustaining waters of her wisdom and healing. We look to her for spiritual guidance to inspire us to celebrate our blessings and work for tikun olam, the repair of the world.

Miriam ha nevi'ah oz v'zimrah beyadah,
Miriam tirkod itanu l'takein et haolam. (2x)
Bimherah v'yameinu hi tevi'enu
El mei hayeshuah. (2x)[27]

Miriam, the prophet,
Dance with us to repair the world.
Bring us soon, your healing waters.

מִרְיָם הַנְּבִיאָה עֹז וְזִמְרָה בְּיָדָהּ.
מִרְיָם תִּרְקוֹד אִתָּנוּ
לְהַגְדִּיל זִמְרַת עוֹלָם
מִרְיָם תִּרְקוֹד אִתָּנוּ
לְתַקֵּן אֶת־הָעוֹלָם.
בִּמְהֵרָה בְיָמֵינוּ הִיא תְּבִיאֵנוּ
אֶל מֵי הַיְשׁוּעָה.

Miriam's Cup represents the living waters that sustained the Hebrews through the wilderness. These were given to the people due to Miriam's merit. Miriam's Well was said to have had healing powers that not only refreshed their bodies, but also renewed their souls. We look to Miriam—prophet, poet, leader, and healer—as a role model, a guide on our spiritual journeys.

Share what nourishes you spiritually.

Welcoming Elijah

*(Pour a cup of wine for Elijah and place it next to
Miriam's Cup at the center of the table.)*

(Some follow the custom of all seder participants, pouring a little wine from
their cups into Elijah's cup, to indicate that each of us must contribute to the
effort to redeem the world. Most Sephardim do not have the custom of opening
the door for Elijah.)

This cup is for Elijah the prophet. We open the door to greet him and invite him
to join us. We pray that he will return to us soon, bringing a time of freedom,
justice and peace for the entire world.

אֵלִיָּהוּ הַנָּבִיא, אֵלִיָּהוּ הַתִּשְׁבִּי,
אֵלִיָּהוּ, אֵלִיָּהוּ, אֵלִיָּהוּ הַגִּלְעָדִי,
בִּמְהֵרָה בְיָמֵינוּ יָבֹא אֵלֵינוּ עִם מָשִׁיחַ בֶּן דָּוִד.

*Eliyahu hanavi, Eliyahu haTishbi,
Eliyahu, Eliyahu, Eliyahu, haGiladi.
Bimheira v'yameinu, yavo eleinu
im Mashiach ben David. (2x)*

May the prophet Elijah, come to us quickly and in our day, bringing the time
of Messiah.

Elijah was both the zealous prophet who demanded vengeance against the wicked Ahab and
Jezebel, as well as the one, according to Malachi, who will "reconcile the hearts of the children
with the hearts of their parents." The rabbis later described him as the one who will usher in the
Messianic era. From Elijah, we learn not to ignore radical evil but also to be open to reconcilia-
tion.

What generational issues do you think now need resolving?

What is your idea of a Messianic time?

Elijah's Chair, Kokand, Uzbekistan, 1999

Palmachim Beach, Israel 2002

WE SING SONGS OF PRAISE

Selected verses from Hallel

God will bless the House of Israel.
God will bless the House of Aaron.
God will bless those who are reverent, young and old alike.

The dead cannot praise God,
nor can those who go down into silence.
But, we shall praise God, now and always.
Halleluyah!

I love to know that God hears my cries.
Because God listens, I will cry out, all the days of my life.

How can I repay God for all the gifts to me?
I will raise the cup of deliverance, and call God by name.
My vows to God will I repay in the presence of all the people.

Thank God for great kindness; God's love endures forever.

Open the gates of righteousness for me,
that I may enter and thank God.
This is the gate of God, the righteous shall
enter here.

This is the day God made;
Let us all rejoice!

לֹא לָנוּ יְיָ לֹא לָנוּ,
עַל חַסְדְּךָ עַל אֲמִתֶּךָ.

כִּי לְשִׁמְךָ תֵּן כָּבוֹד,

לָמָּה יֹאמְרוּ הַגּוֹיִם,
וֵאלֹהֵינוּ בַשָּׁמַיִם
עֲצַבֵּיהֶם כֶּסֶף וְזָהָב,
פֶּה לָהֶם וְלֹא יְדַבֵּרוּ,
אָזְנַיִם לָהֶם וְלֹא יִשְׁמָעוּ,
יְדֵיהֶם וְלֹא יְמִישׁוּן,

אַיֵּה נָא אֱלֹהֵיהֶם.
כֹּל אֲשֶׁר חָפֵץ עָשָׂה.
מַעֲשֵׂה יְדֵי אָדָם.
עֵינַיִם לָהֶם וְלֹא יִרְאוּ.
אַף לָהֶם וְלֹא יְרִיחוּן.
רַגְלֵיהֶם וְלֹא יְהַלֵּכוּ,

לֹא יֶהְגּוּ בִּגְרוֹנָם.

כְּמוֹהֶם יִהְיוּ עֹשֵׂיהֶם,
יִשְׂרָאֵל בְּטַח בַּיָי,
בֵּית אַהֲרֹן בִּטְחוּ בַיָי,
יִרְאֵי יְיָ בִּטְחוּ בַיָי,

כֹּל אֲשֶׁר בֹּטֵחַ בָּהֶם:
עֶזְרָם וּמָגִנָּם הוּא.
עֶזְרָם וּמָגִנָּם הוּא.
עֶזְרָם וּמָגִנָּם הוּא.

יְיָ זְכָרָנוּ יְבָרֵךְ,
יְבָרֵךְ אֶת בֵּית אַהֲרֹן.
יְבָרֵךְ יִרְאֵי יְיָ,
יֹסֵף יְיָ עֲלֵיכֶם,
בְּרוּכִים אַתֶּם לַיָי,
הַשָּׁמַיִם שָׁמַיִם לַיָי,
לֹא הַמֵּתִים יְהַלְלוּ יָהּ,
וַאֲנַחְנוּ נְבָרֵךְ יָהּ,

יְבָרֵךְ אֶת בֵּית יִשְׂרָאֵל,

הַקְּטַנִּים עִם הַגְּדֹלִים.
עֲלֵיכֶם וְעַל בְּנֵיכֶם.
עֹשֵׂה שָׁמַיִם וָאָרֶץ.
וְהָאָרֶץ נָתַן לִבְנֵי אָדָם.
וְלֹא כָּל יֹרְדֵי דוּמָה.
מֵעַתָּה וְעַד עוֹלָם, הַלְלוּיָהּ:

אָהַבְתִּי כִּי יִשְׁמַע יְיָ,
כִּי הִטָּה אָזְנוֹ לִי
אֲפָפוּנִי חֶבְלֵי מָוֶת,

אֶת קוֹלִי תַּחֲנוּנָי.
וּבְיָמַי אֶקְרָא:
וּמְצָרֵי שְׁאוֹל מְצָאוּנִי

צָרָה וְיָגוֹן אֶמְצָא.

וּבְשֵׁם יְיָ אֶקְרָא,
חַנּוּן יְיָ וְצַדִּיק,
שֹׁמֵר פְּתָאִים יְיָ

אָנָּה יְיָ מַלְּטָה נַפְשִׁי.
וֵאלֹהֵינוּ מְרַחֵם.
דַּלּוֹתִי וְלִי יְהוֹשִׁיעַ.

שׁוּבִי נַפְשִׁי לִמְנוּחָיְכִי,   כִּי יְיָ גָּמַל עָלָיְכִי.
כִּי חִלַּצְתָּ נַפְשִׁי מִמָּוֶת   אֶת עֵינִי מִן דִּמְעָה,
אֶת רַגְלִי מִדֶּחִי.

אֶתְהַלֵּךְ לִפְנֵי יְיָ,   בְּאַרְצוֹת הַחַיִּים.
הֶאֱמַנְתִּי כִּי אֲדַבֵּר,   אֲנִי עָנִיתִי מְאֹד.
אֲנִי אָמַרְתִּי בְחָפְזִי   כָּל הָאָדָם כֹּזֵב.

מָה אָשִׁיב לַיְיָ,   כָּל תַּגְמוּלוֹהִי עָלָי.
כּוֹס יְשׁוּעוֹת אֶשָּׂא,   וּבְשֵׁם יְיָ אֶקְרָא.
נְדָרַי לַיְיָ אֲשַׁלֵּם,   נֶגְדָה נָּא לְכָל עַמּוֹ.
יָקָר בְּעֵינֵי יְיָ   הַמָּוְתָה לַחֲסִידָיו.
אָנָּה יְיָ כִּי אֲנִי עַבְדֶּךָ   אֲנִי עַבְדְּךָ, בֶּן אֲמָתֶךָ
פִּתַּחְתָּ לְמוֹסֵרָי.

לְךָ אֶזְבַּח זֶבַח תּוֹדָה   וּבְשֵׁם יְיָ אֶקְרָא.
נְדָרַי לַיְיָ אֲשַׁלֵּם   נֶגְדָה נָּא לְכָל עַמּוֹ.
בְּחַצְרוֹת בֵּית יְיָ   בְּתוֹכֵכִי יְרוּשָׁלָיִם הַלְלוּיָהּ.

הַלְלוּ אֶת יְיָ, כָּל גּוֹיִם,   שַׁבְּחוּהוּ כָּל הָאֻמִּים.
כִּי גָבַר עָלֵינוּ חַסְדּוֹ,   וֶאֱמֶת יְיָ לְעוֹלָם הַלְלוּיָהּ:

הוֹדוּ לַיְיָ כִּי טוֹב,   כִּי לְעוֹלָם חַסְדּוֹ:
יֹאמַר נָא יִשְׂרָאֵל,   כִּי לְעוֹלָם חַסְדּוֹ:
יֹאמְרוּ נָא בֵית אַהֲרֹן,   כִּי לְעוֹלָם חַסְדּוֹ:
יֹאמְרוּ נָא יִרְאֵי יְיָ,   כִּי לְעוֹלָם חַסְדּוֹ:

מִן הַמֵּצַר קָרָאתִי יָּהּ,   עָנָנִי בַמֶּרְחָב יָהּ.
יְיָ לִי לֹא אִירָא,   מַה יַּעֲשֶׂה לִי אָדָם.
יְיָ לִי בְּעֹזְרָי,   וַאֲנִי אֶרְאֶה בְשֹׂנְאָי.
טוֹב לַחֲסוֹת בַּיְיָ,   מִבְּטֹחַ בָּאָדָם.
טוֹב לַחֲסוֹת בַּיְיָ   מִבְּטֹחַ בִּנְדִיבִים.
כָּל גּוֹיִם סְבָבוּנִי   בְּשֵׁם יְיָ כִּי אֲמִילַם.
סַבּוּנִי גַם סְבָבוּנִי   בְּשֵׁם יְיָ כִּי אֲמִילַם.
סַבּוּנִי כִדְבֹרִים   דֹּעֲכוּ כְּאֵשׁ קוֹצִים,

בְּשֵׁם יְיָ כִּי אֲמִילַם.

דָּחֹה דְחִיתַנִי לִנְפֹּל,   וַיְיָ עֲזָרָנִי.

עָזִּי וְזִמְרָת יָהּ,   וַיְהִי לִי לִישׁוּעָה.

קוֹל רִנָּה וִישׁוּעָה   בְּאָהֳלֵי צַדִּיקִים,

יְמִין יְיָ עֹשָׂה חָיִל.

יְמִין יְיָ רוֹמֵמָה,   יְמִין יְיָ עֹשָׂה חָיִל.

לֹא אָמוּת כִּי אֶחְיֶה,   וַאֲסַפֵּר מַעֲשֵׂי יָהּ.

יַסֹּר יִסְּרַנִּי יָּהּ,   וְלַמָּוֶת לֹא נְתָנָנִי.

פִּתְחוּ לִי שַׁעֲרֵי צֶדֶק,   אָבֹא בָם אוֹדֶה יָהּ.

זֶה הַשַּׁעַר לַיְיָ,   צַדִּיקִים יָבֹאוּ בוֹ.

אוֹדְךָ כִּי עֲנִיתָנִי,   וַתְּהִי לִי לִישׁוּעָה.

אוֹדְךָ כִּי עֲנִיתָנִי,   וַתְּהִי לִי לִישׁוּעָה.

אֶבֶן מָאֲסוּ הַבּוֹנִים,   הָיְתָה לְ[רֹ]אשׁ פִּנָּה.

אֶבֶן מָאֲסוּ הַבּוֹנִים,   הָיְתָה לְ[רֹ]אשׁ פִּנָּה.

מֵאֵת יְיָ הָיְתָה זֹּאת,   הִיא נִפְלָאת בְּעֵינֵינוּ:

מֵאֵת יְיָ הָיְתָה זֹּאת,   הִיא נִפְלָאת בְּעֵינֵינוּ.

זֶה הַיּוֹם עָשָׂה יְיָ,   נָגִילָה וְנִשְׂמְחָה בוֹ.

זֶה הַיּוֹם עָשָׂה יְיָ   נָגִילָה וְנִשְׂמְחָה בוֹ.

אָנָּא יְיָ הוֹשִׁיעָה נָּא: אָנָּא יְיָ הוֹשִׁיעָה נָּא:

אָנָּא יְיָ הַצְלִיחָה נָּא: אָנָּא יְיָ הַצְלִיחָה נָּא:

בָּרוּךְ הַבָּא בְּשֵׁם יְיָ,   בֵּרַכְנוּכֶם מִבֵּית יְיָ.

בָּרוּךְ הַבָּא בְּשֵׁם יְיָ,   בֵּרַכְנוּכֶם מִבֵּית יְיָ.

אֵל יְיָ וַיָּאֶר לָנוּ,   אִסְרוּ חַג בַּעֲבֹתִים

עַד קַרְנוֹת הַמִּזְבֵּחַ.

אֵלִי אַתָּה וְאוֹדֶךָ,   אֱלֹהַי אֲרוֹמְמֶךָּ.

הוֹדוּ לַיְיָ כִּי טוֹב,   כִּי לְעוֹלָם חַסְדּוֹ.

יְהַלְלוּךָ יְיָ אֱלֹהֵינוּ כָּל מַעֲשֶׂיךָ, וַחֲסִידֶיךָ צַדִּיקִים עוֹשֵׂי רְצוֹנֶךָ, וְכָל עַמְּךָ בֵּית יִשְׂרָאֵל בְּרִנָּה יוֹדוּ וִיבָרְכוּ וִישַׁבְּחוּ וִיפָאֲרוּ וִירוֹמְמוּ וְיַעֲרִיצוּ וְיַקְדִּישׁוּ וְיַמְלִיכוּ אֶת שִׁמְךָ מַלְכֵּנוּ, כִּי לְךָ טוֹב לְהוֹדוֹת וּלְשִׁמְךָ נָאֶה לְזַמֵּר, כִּי מֵעוֹלָם וְעַד עוֹלָם אַתָּה אֵל. בָּרוּךְ אַתָּה יְיָ, מֶלֶךְ מְהֻלָּל בַּתִּשְׁבָּחוֹת.

Count the Omer
(second night only)

Passover is both an historical festival celebrating the Exodus from Egypt and an agricultural holiday marking the beginning of the barley harvest.

On the second day of Passover, an omer, a sheaf of barley, was brought to the Temple in Jerusalem as an offering. Shavuot, which comes 49 days later, marks the beginning of the wheat harvest.

Shavuot is also the time of the giving of the Torah. We count the 49 days until this festival to show the connection—that our freedom was not complete until we received the Torah. At Sinai, we switched our allegiance from a human ruler to becoming "servants of God."

(Count the Omer with the blessing.)

בָּרוּךְ אַתָּה יי אֱלֹהֵינוּ מֶלֶךְ הָעוֹלָם אֲשֶׁר קִדְּשָׁנוּ בְּמִצְוֹתָיו וְצִוָּנוּ עַל סְפִירַת הָעֹמֶר. הַיּוֹם יוֹם אֶחָד לָעֹמֶר.

Baruch Atah Adonai, Eloheinu melech haolam, asher kid'shanu b'mitzvotav, v'tzivanu al sefirat ha'omer. Hayom yom echad la'omer.

Blessed are You, Adonai our God, Sovereign of the world, who made us holy by Your mitzvot and commanded us to count the Omer.

Today is the First Day of the Omer.

Help the children make a decorative Omer Calendar to "count down" the days from Passover to Shavuot. Each night, have family members count their blessings and choose a mitzvah to do each day.

Make a special Omer Tzedakah Box in which to place coins each day of the Omer period (except for holidays and Shabbat.) The total can be donated to an organization that provides food for the poor or infirm elderly.

Renovation, Eldridge Street Synagogue, New York City, USA 1985

Folk Singer, Tashkent, Uzbekistan, 1998

SEDER SONGS

Adir Hu (Mighty Is God) אַדִּיר הוּא

אַדִּיר הוּא, אַדִּיר הוּא, יִבְנֶה בֵיתוֹ בְּקָרוֹב, בִּמְהֵרָה בִּמְהֵרָה, בְּיָמֵינוּ בְּקָרוֹב. אֵל בְּנֵה, בְּנֵה בֵיתְךָ בְּקָרוֹב.

בָּחוּר הוּא, גָּדוֹל הוּא, דָּגוּל הוּא, יִבְנֶה בֵיתוֹ בְּקָרוֹב, בִּמְהֵרָה בִּמְהֵרָה, בְּיָמֵינוּ בְּקָרוֹב. אֵל בְּנֵה, אֵל בְּנֵה, בְּנֵה בֵיתְךָ בְּקָרוֹב.

הָדוּר הוּא, וָתִיק הוּא, זַכַּאי הוּא, חָסִיד הוּא, יִבְנֶה בֵיתוֹ בְּקָרוֹב, בִּמְהֵרָה בִּמְהֵרָה, בְּיָמֵינוּ בְּקָרוֹב. אֵל בְּנֵה, אֵל בְּנֵה, בְּנֵה בֵיתְךָ בְּקָרוֹב.

טָהוֹר הוּא, יָחִיד הוּא, כַּבִּיר הוּא, לָמוּד הוּא, מֶלֶךְ הוּא, נוֹרָא הוּא, סַגִּיב הוּא, עִזּוּז הוּא, פּוֹדֶה הוּא, צַדִּיק הוּא, יִבְנֶה בֵיתוֹ בְּקָרוֹב, בִּמְהֵרָה בִּמְהֵרָה, בְּיָמֵינוּ בְּקָרוֹב. אֵל בְּנֵה, אֵל בְּנֵה, בְּנֵה בֵיתְךָ בְּקָרוֹב.

קָדוֹשׁ הוּא, רַחוּם הוּא, שַׁדַּי הוּא, תַּקִּיף הוּא, יִבְנֶה בֵיתוֹ בְּקָרוֹב, בִּמְהֵרָה בִּמְהֵרָה, בְּיָמֵינוּ בְּקָרוֹב. אֵל בְּנֵה, אֵל בְּנֵה, בְּנֵה בֵיתְךָ בְּקָרוֹב.

*Adir hu, adir hu, yivneh veito b'karov, bimheirah, bimheirah, b'yameinu b'karov.
Eil b'nai, Eil b'nei , b'nei vetcha b'karov.*

*Bachur hu, gadol hu, dagul hu...
Hadur hu, vatik hu, zakai hu, chassid hu...
Tahor hu, yahid hu, kabir hu, lamud hu, melech hu...
Nora hu, sagiv hu, izuz hu, podeh hu, tzadik hu ...
Kadosh hu, rachum hu, shadai hu, takif hu...*

Mighty is God
May God's kingdom be established speedily and in our lifetime.

God is chosen, great, renowned, glorious, faithful, just, pious, pure, unique, powerful, knowing, majestic, awesome, exalted, potent, redeeming, righteous, holy, merciful, sustaining, and forceful.

Adir Hu lists attributes of God following the Hebrew alphabet. Go around the room, each saying your own attribute, following the English alphabet. For example, Awesome is God, Blessed is God, Comforting is God and so forth.

Echad Mi Yodea?   אֶחָד מִי יוֹדֵעַ?

אֶחָד מִי יוֹדֵעַ? אֶחָד אֲנִי יוֹדֵעַ: אֶחָד
אֱלֹהֵינוּ שֶׁבַּשָּׁמַיִם וּבָאָרֶץ.
שְׁנַיִם מִי יוֹדֵעַ? שְׁנַיִם אֲנִי יוֹדֵעַ: שְׁנֵי
לֻחוֹת הַבְּרִית, אֶחָד אֱלֹהֵינוּ שֶׁבַּשָּׁמַיִם
וּבָאָרֶץ.

תִּשְׁעָה יַרְחֵי לֵדָה, שְׁמוֹנָה יְמֵי מִילָה,
צְמִיחַ שַׁבַּתָּא, שִׁשָּׁה סִדְרֵי מִשְׁנָה,
חֲמִשָּׁה חוּמְשֵׁי תוֹרָה, אַרְבַּע אִמָּהוֹת,
שְׁלֹשָׁה אָבוֹת, שְׁנֵי לֻחוֹת הַבְּרִית, אֶחָד
אֱלֹהֵינוּ שֶׁבַּשָּׁמַיִם וּבָאָרֶץ.

שְׁלֹשָׁה מִי יוֹדֵעַ? שְׁלֹשָׁה אֲנִי יוֹדֵעַ:
שְׁלֹשָׁה אָבוֹת, שְׁנֵי לֻחוֹת הַבְּרִית, אֶחָד
אֱלֹהֵינוּ שֶׁבַּשָּׁמַיִם וּבָאָרֶץ.

עֲשָׂרָה מִי יוֹדֵעַ? עֲשָׂרָה אֲנִי יוֹדֵעַ: עֲשָׂרָה
דִבְּרַיָּא, תִּשְׁעָה יַרְחֵי לֵדָה, שְׁמוֹנָה יְמֵי
מִילָה, שִׁבְעָה יְמֵי שַׁבַּתָּא, שִׁשָּׁה סִדְרֵי
מִשְׁנָה, חֲמִשָּׁה חוּמְשֵׁי תוֹרָה, אַרְבַּע
אִמָּהוֹת, שְׁלֹשָׁה אָבוֹת, שְׁנֵי לֻחוֹת
הַבְּרִית, אֶחָד אֱלֹהֵינוּ שֶׁבַּשָּׁמַיִם וּבָאָרֶץ.

אַרְבַּע מִי יוֹדֵעַ? אַרְבַּע אֲנִי יוֹדֵעַ: אַרְבַּע
אִמָּהוֹת, שְׁלֹשָׁה אָבוֹת, שְׁנֵי לֻחוֹת
הַבְּרִית, אֶחָד אֱלֹהֵינוּ שֶׁבַּשָּׁמַיִם וּבָאָרֶץ.

אַחַד עָשָׂר מִי יוֹדֵעַ? אַחַד עָשָׂר אֲנִי
יוֹדֵעַ: אַחַד עָשָׂר כּוֹכְבַיָּא, עֲשָׂרָה
דִבְּרַיָּא, תִּשְׁעָה יַרְחֵי לֵדָה, שְׁמוֹנָה יְמֵי
מִילָה, שִׁבְעָה יְמֵי שַׁבַּתָּא, שִׁשָּׁה סִדְרֵי
מִשְׁנָה, חֲמִשָּׁה חוּמְשֵׁי תוֹרָה, אַרְבַּע
אִמָּהוֹת, שְׁלֹשָׁה אָבוֹת, שְׁנֵי לֻחוֹת
הַבְּרִית, אֶחָד אֱלֹהֵינוּ שֶׁבַּשָּׁמַיִם וּבָאָרֶץ.

חֲמִשָּׁה מִי יוֹדֵעַ? חֲמִשָּׁה אֲנִי יוֹדֵעַ:
חֲמִשָּׁה חוּמְשֵׁי תוֹרָה, אַרְבַּע אִמָּהוֹת,
שְׁלֹשָׁה אָבוֹת, שְׁנֵי לֻחוֹת הַבְּרִית, אֶחָד
אֱלֹהֵינוּ שֶׁבַּשָּׁמַיִם וּבָאָרֶץ.

שִׁשָּׁה מִי יוֹדֵעַ? שִׁשָּׁה אֲנִי יוֹדֵעַ: שִׁשָּׁה
סִדְרֵי מִשְׁנָה, חֲמִשָּׁה חוּמְשֵׁי תוֹרָה,
אַרְבַּע אִמָּהוֹת, שְׁלֹשָׁה אָבוֹת, שְׁנֵי לֻחוֹת
הַבְּרִית, אֶחָד אֱלֹהֵינוּ שֶׁבַּשָּׁמַיִם וּבָאָרֶץ.

שְׁנֵים עָשָׂר מִי יוֹדֵעַ? שְׁנֵים עָשָׂר אֲנִי
יוֹדֵעַ: שְׁנֵים עָשָׂר שִׁבְטַיָּא, אַחַד עָשָׂר
כּוֹכְבַיָּא, עֲשָׂרָה דִבְּרַיָּא, תִּשְׁעָה יַרְחֵי
לֵדָה, שְׁמוֹנָה יְמֵי מִילָה, שִׁבְעָה יְמֵי
שַׁבַּתָּא, שִׁשָּׁה סִדְרֵי מִשְׁנָה, חֲמִשָּׁה
חוּמְשֵׁי תוֹרָה, אַרְבַּע אִמָּהוֹת, שְׁלֹשָׁה
אָבוֹת, שְׁנֵי לֻחוֹת הַבְּרִית, אֶחָד אֱלֹהֵינוּ
שֶׁבַּשָּׁמַיִם וּבָאָרֶץ.

שִׁבְעָה מִי יוֹדֵעַ? שִׁבְעָה אֲנִי יוֹדֵעַ: שִׁבְעָה
יְמֵי שַׁבַּתָּא, שִׁשָּׁה סִדְרֵי מִשְׁנָה, חֲמִשָּׁה
חוּמְשֵׁי תוֹרָה, אַרְבַּע אִמָּהוֹת, שְׁלֹשָׁה
אָבוֹת, שְׁנֵי לֻחוֹת הַבְּרִית, אֶחָד אֱלֹהֵינוּ
שֶׁבַּשָּׁמַיִם וּבָאָרֶץ.

שְׁלֹשָׁה עָשָׂר מִי יוֹדֵעַ? שְׁלֹשָׁה עָשָׂר אֲנִי
יוֹדֵעַ: שְׁלֹשָׁה עָשָׂר מִדַּיָּא, שְׁנֵים עָשָׂר
שִׁבְטַיָּא, אַחַד עָשָׂר כּוֹכְבַיָּא, עֲשָׂרָה
דִבְּרַיָּא, תִּשְׁעָה יַרְחֵי לֵדָה, שְׁמוֹנָה יְמֵי
מִילָה, שִׁבְעָה יְמֵי שַׁבַּתָּא, שִׁשָּׁה סִדְרֵי
מִשְׁנָה, חֲמִשָּׁה חוּמְשֵׁי תוֹרָה, אַרְבַּע
אִמָּהוֹת, שְׁלֹשָׁה אָבוֹת, שְׁנֵי לֻחוֹת
הַבְּרִית, אֶחָד אֱלֹהֵינוּ שֶׁבַּשָּׁמַיִם וּבָאָרֶץ.

שְׁמוֹנָה מִי יוֹדֵעַ? שְׁמוֹנָה אֲנִי יוֹדֵעַ:
שְׁמוֹנָה יְמֵי מִילָה, שִׁבְעָה יְמֵי שַׁבַּתָּא,
שִׁשָּׁה סִדְרֵי מִשְׁנָה, חֲמִשָּׁה חוּמְשֵׁי
תוֹרָה, אַרְבַּע אִמָּהוֹת, שְׁלֹשָׁה אָבוֹת,
שְׁנֵי לֻחוֹת הַבְּרִית, אֶחָד אֱלֹהֵינוּ
שֶׁבַּשָּׁמַיִם וּבָאָרֶץ.

תִּשְׁעָה מִי יוֹדֵעַ? תִּשְׁעָה אֲנִי יוֹדֵעַ:

Echad Mi Yodea?
Who Knows One?

(As you sing each new verse, add the ones you previously sang.)

Echad Mi Yodea?

Echad mi yodea? Echad ani yodea!
Echad Eloheinu, sh'bashamayim uva'aretz

Shnei luchot habrit, shlosha avot, arba imahot, chamisha chumshei Torah,
shisha sidrei Mishna, shiv'ah y'mai shabata, shmonah y'mai milah, tishah
yarchei leidah, asarah debraiyah, achad asar kochvaiya, shenem asar shivtai-
ya, shlosha asar midaiya

Who Knows One?

Who knows 1?	I know 1!	One is our God in the heaven and earth.
Who knows 2?	I know 2!	There are 2 tablets of the law.
Who knows 3?	I know 3!	There are 3 fathers.
Who knows 4?	I know 4!	There are 4 mothers.
Who knows 5?	I know 5!	There are 5 books of the Torah.
Who knows 6?	I know 6!	There are 6 books of Mishna.
Who knows 7?	I know 7!	There are 7 days of the week.
Who knows 8?	I know 8!	There are 8 days to circumcision.
Who knows 9?	I know 9!	There are 9 months of pregnancy.
Who knows 10?	I know 10!	There are 10 commandments.
Who knows 11?	I know 11!	There are 11 stars in Joseph's dream.
Who knows 12?	I know 12!	There are 12 tribes.
Who knows 13?	I know 13!	There are 13 attributes of God.

Echad Mi Yodeah is a most appropriate song to sing because this is a night of numbers and calculations. The song also enumerates the basic elements of our faith and tradition. The song has a special appeal to children and helps keep them awake!

Have "certificates" ready for children who knew the correct answers or were able to stay up to sing this song, or who could sing all the verses rapidly.

Ask a different participant to answer each question. As the song repeats, each says his/her part. Add motions to add to the fun.

Chad Gadya חַד גַּדְיָא
(One Only Kid)

(As you add each character, repeat all that has thus far been sung, so the song increases with each verse, whether in Hebrew or English. Add the chorus after each verse.)

חַד גַּדְיָא, חַד גַּדְיָא
דְּזַבִּין אַבָּא בִּתְרֵי זוּזֵי, חַד
גַּדְיָא, חַד גַּדְיָא.

וְאָתָא שׁוּנְרָא, וְאָכְלָה לְגַדְיָא,
דְּזַבִּין אַבָּא בִּתְרֵי זוּזֵי, חַד
גַּדְיָא, חַד גַּדְיָא.

וְאָתָא כַלְבָּא, וְנָשַׁךְ לְשׁוּנְרָא,
דְּאָכְלָה לְגַדְיָא, דְּזַבִּין אַבָּא
בִּתְרֵי זוּזֵי, חַד גַּדְיָא, חַד גַּדְיָא.

וְאָתָא חוּטְרָא, וְהִכָּה לְכַלְבָּא,
דְּנָשַׁךְ לְשׁוּנְרָא, דְּאָכְלָה
לְגַדְיָא, דְּזַבִּין אַבָּא בִּתְרֵי זוּזֵי,
חַד גַּדְיָא, חַד גַּדְיָא.

וְאָתָא נוּרָא, וְשָׂרַף לְחוּטְרָא,
דְּהִכָּה לְכַלְבָּא, דְּנָשַׁךְ
לְשׁוּנְרָא, דְּאָכְלָה לְגַדְיָא,
דְּזַבִּין אַבָּא בִּתְרֵי זוּזֵי, חַד
גַּדְיָא, חַד גַּדְיָא.

וְאָתָא מַיָּא, וְכָבָה לְנוּרָא,
דְּשָׂרַף לְחוּטְרָא, דְּהִכָּה
לְכַלְבָּא, דְּנָשַׁךְ לְשׁוּנְרָא,
דְּאָכְלָה לְגַדְיָא, דְּזַבִּין אַבָּא
בִּתְרֵי זוּזֵי, חַד גַּדְיָא, חַד
גַּדְיָא. וְאָתָא תוֹרָא, וְשָׁתָא

לְמַיָּא, דְּכָבָה לְנוּרָא, דְּשָׂרַף
לְחוּטְרָא, דְּהִכָּה לְכַלְבָּא,
דְּנָשַׁךְ לְשׁוּנְרָא, דְּאָכְלָה
לְגַדְיָא, דְּזַבִּין אַבָּא בִּתְרֵי זוּזֵי,
חַד גַּדְיָא, חַד גַּדְיָא.

וְאָתָא הַשּׁוֹחֵט, וְשָׁחַט לְתוֹרָא,
דְּשָׁתָא לְמַיָּא, דְּכָבָה לְנוּרָא,
דְּשָׂרַף לְחוּטְרָא,דְּהִכָּה
לְכַלְבָּא, דְּנָשַׁךְ לְשׁוּנְרָא,
דְּאָכְלָה לְגַדְיָא, דְּזַבִּין אַבָּא
בִּתְרֵי זוּזֵי, חַד גַּדְיָא, חַד גַּדְיָא.

וְאָתָא מַלְאַךְ הַמָּוֶת, וְשָׁחַט
לְשׁוֹחֵט, דְּשָׁחַט לְתוֹרָא,
דְּשָׁתָא לְמַיָּא, דְּכָבָה לְנוּרָא,
דְּשָׂרַף לְחוּטְרָא,דְּהִכָּה
לְכַלְבָּא, דְּנָשַׁךְ לְשׁוּנְרָא,
דְּאָכְלָה לְגַדְיָא, דְּזַבִּין אַבָּא
בִּתְרֵי זוּזֵי, חַד גַּדְיָא, חַד גַּדְיָא.

וְאָתָא הַקָּדוֹשׁ בָּרוּךְ הוּא,
וְשָׁחַט לְמַלְאַךְ הַמָּוֶת, דְּשָׁחַט
לְתוֹרָא, דְּשָׁתָא לְמַיָּא, דְּכָבָה
לְנוּרָא, דְּשָׂרַף לְחוּטְרָא,
דְּהִכָּה לְכַלְבָּא, דְּנָשַׁךְ
לְשׁוּנְרָא, דְּאָכְלָה לְגַדְיָא,
דְּזַבִּין אַבָּא בִּתְרֵי זוּזֵי, חַד
גַּדְיָא, חַד גַּדְיָא.

Chad Gadya

Introduction
Chad Gadya, chad Gadya
D'zabin abba bit'trei zuzei,
Chad Gadya, chad Gadya.

Chorus
D'zabin abba bit'rei zuzei
Chad Gadya, chad gadya.

One Only Kid

Introduction
One only kid, one only kid
that my father bought for two zuzim.
One only kid, one only kid.

Chorus
that my father bought for two zuzim.
One only kid, one only kid.

Shochet, Rosh Ha'ayin, Israel, 1983

Along came a cat and ate the kid…
Along came a dog and bit the cat…
Along came a stick and beat the dog…
Along came a fire and burnt the stick…
Along came water and put out the fire…
Along came an ox and drank the water…
Along came a butcher and slaughtered the ox…
Along came the angel of death and slew the butcher…
Along came the Holy One and killed the angel of death…

In this song, written in Aramaic, the Jewish people is compared to an innocent lamb that the parent purchased for two zuzim, which stands for the Ten Commandments, the two tablets of the law. We are set upon by many enemies—the cat is Assyria, the dog is Babylonia, the stick is Persia, the fire is Greece, the water is Rome, the ox is the Saracens, the butcher is the crusaders, the angel of death is the Ottomans. In the end, they devour each other. The song ends with an expression of hope that God will bring peace and eternal life to the people Israel.

Have children make hand puppets or pictures to display at the appropriate parts of the song.

We sing the song quickly because we don't want to dwell on the bad, but want to reach the happy ending. The last verse is traditionally sung slowly.

What do we need to do to ensure Jewish survival?

New Immigrants, Ben Guryon Airport, Israel, 1996

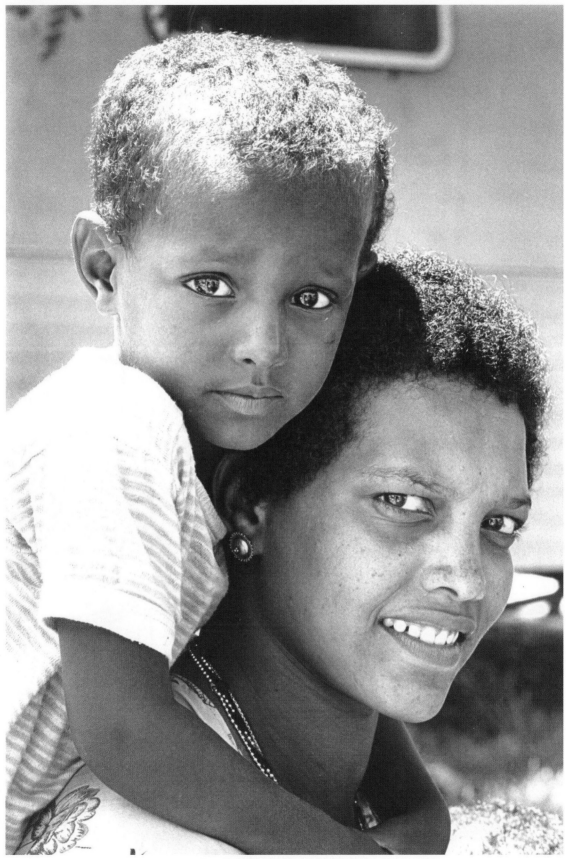

Mother and Son, Ramla, Israel 1986

Fringes, Jewish Quarter, Jerusalem, Israel 1984

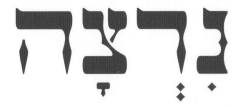

COMPLETE THE SEDER

The Fourth Cup – "I Will Take You To Be My People"

We are now ready for the fourth cup of wine, which we drink while reclining.

Baruch Atah Adonai, Eloheinu melech haolam, borei p'ree ha gafen.

בָּרוּךְ אַתָּה יְיָ, אֱלֹהֵינוּ מֶלֶךְ הָעוֹלָם, בּוֹרֵא פְּרִי הַגָּפֶן:

Blessed are You Adonai, Sovereign of the world, who creates the fruit of the vine.

(Drink the fourth cup while reclining.)

Chasal siddur Pesach k'hilchato	חֲסַל סִדּוּר פֶּסַח כְּהִלְכָתוֹ,
K'chol mishpato v'chukato.	כְּכָל מִשְׁפָּטוֹ וְחֻקָּתוֹ.
Ka'asher zachinu l'sader oto	כַּאֲשֶׁר זָכִינוּ לְסַדֵּר אוֹתוֹ,
Ken nizkeh la'asoto.	כֵּן נִזְכֶּה לַעֲשׂוֹתוֹ.
Zach shochen m'onah	זָךְ שׁוֹכֵן מְעוֹנָה,
Komem k'hal adat mi manah.	קוֹמֵם קְהַל עֲדַת מִי מָנָה.
B'karov nahel nitei chanah	בְּקָרוֹב נַהֵל נִטְעֵי כַנָּה,
P'duyim l'Zion b'rina.	פְּדוּיִם לְצִיּוֹן בְּרִנָּה.

(The Passover seder can set the tone for one's spirituality throughout the year. Thus we pray that all we have arranged for this night, all of our "spiritual plantings", bear fruit.)

Our seder is now completed. We have fulfilled every law and custom.
As we celebrated this year, may we be granted the blessing of celebrating Passover for many years to come. Pure and Holy One, Transcendent and Immanent God, Raise up Your people with love and lead us to Zion in joyful song.

לְשָׁנָה הַבָּאָה בִּירוּשָׁלָיִם.

Lashana haba'ah b'Yerushalayim!

NEXT YEAR IN JERUSALEM!

In our time, some suggest that we drink a fifth cup of wine to celebrate the establishment of The State of Israel. It is an appropriate time to sing Hatikvah, the Jewish National Anthem.

Hatikvah התִּקְוָה

כָּל־עוֹד בַּלֵּבָב פְּנִימָה, נֶפֶשׁ יְהוּדִי הוֹמִיָּה,
וּלְפַאֲתֵי מִזְרָח קָדִימָה, עַיִן לְצִיּוֹן צוֹפִיָּה.
עוֹד לֹא אָבְדָה תִקְוָתֵנוּ, הַתִּקְוָה בַּת שְׁנוֹת אַלְפַּיִם
לִהְיוֹת עַם חָפְשִׁי בְּאַרְצֵנוּ, אֶרֶץ צִיּוֹן וִירוּשָׁלָיִם.

Kol od balevav p'nimah, Nefesh Yehudi homiyah.
Ul'fatei mizrach kadimah, Ayin l'tzion tzofiyah.
Od lo avdah tikvatenu, Hatikvah, bat sh'not alpayim
Li'yot am chofshi b'artzenu, Eretz Tzion V'Yerushalyim.
(Repeat last two lines)

What is your hope for Israel? The Jewish people? The world?

Some end the seder singing Ani Ma'amin, the words of the 12th century scholar, Maimonodes, or the poem Halikha Le'Kesaria (Eli, Eli), by Hannah Senesh, a young woman who was killed by the Nazis after she parachuted into Nazi territory in order to rescue Jewish children and bring them to Israel.

Ani Ma'amin אֲנִי מַאֲמִין

אֲנִי מַאֲמִין, אֲנִי מַאֲמִין, אֲנִי מַאֲמִין, בְּאֱמוּנָה שְׁלֵמָה,
בְּבִיאַת הַמָּשִׁיחַ, בְּבִיאַת הַמָּשִׁיחַ אֲנִי מַאֲמִין,
וְאַף־עַל־פִּי שֶׁיִּתְמַהְמַהּ, עִם כָּל זֶה אֲנִי מַאֲמִין

Ani ma'amin, ani ma'min, ani ma'amin, b'emunah sh'leima,
B'viat ha mashiach, b'viat ha mashiach ani ma'amin.
V'afalpi sh'yitmahamah, im kol zeh ani ma'amin.

I believe with all my heart in the coming of the Messiah. And even though the Messiah tarries, I still believe.

Halikha Le'Kesaria (Eli, Eli)

Eli, Eli, Sh'lo yigamer l'olam
Hachol v'hayam
Rishrush shel ha mayim
Barak ha shamayim
Tefilat ha'adam.

הַלִיכָה לְקֵיסָרְיָה (אֵלִי, אֵלִי)

אֵלִי, אֵלִי, שֶׁלֹּא יִגָּמֵר לְעוֹלָם
הַחוֹל וְהַיָּם,
רִשְׁרוּשׁ שֶׁל הַמַּיִם,
בְּרַק הַשָּׁמַיִם,
תְּפִלַּת הָאָדָם.

My God, my God, may these never end: the sand and the sea, the sound of the waters, the thunder of the heavens, the prayers of humanity.

Following the seder, there is a custom among some Sephardim to take the charoset and put it in five places, symbolizing the Chamsa (God's protective hand) at the entrance to the house.

Jewish Day School, Bukhara, Uzbekistan 1999.

Song of Songs

Some have the custom of staying up all night, since the Hebrews did not sleep during the night of the Exodus. Besides elaborating on the story, many recite Song of Songs to express the mutual love of God and the Jewish people.

Selections from Song of Songs

—Give me the kisses of your mouth, for your love is more delightful than wine.

—Like a lily among thorns, so is my darling among the maidens.

—Like an apple tree among the oak in the forest, so is my beloved among the youths.

—Sustain me with raisin cakes, refresh me with apples, for I am faint with love.

—My dove in the cranny of the rocks, hidden by the cliff, let me see your face, let me hear your voice; for your voice is sweet and your face comely.

—My beloved is mine and I am his who browses among the lilies.

—Let me be a seal upon your heart, like the seal upon your hand.

—Hurry my beloved, swift as a gazelle or a young stag, to the hills of spices!

Old Age Home, Montevideo, Uruguay, 2002

מִתּוֹךְ שִׁיר הַשִּׁירִים

יִשָּׁקֵנִי מִנְּשִׁיקוֹת פִּיהוּ, כִּי־טוֹבִים דֹּדֶיךָ מִיָּיִן.

כְּשׁוֹשַׁנָּה בֵּין הַחוֹחִים, כֵּן רַעְיָתִי בֵּין הַבָּנוֹת.

כְּתַפּוּחַ בַּעֲצֵי הַיַּעַר, כֵּן דּוֹדִי בֵּין הַבָּנִים.

סַמְּכוּנִי, בָּאֲשִׁישׁוֹת רַפְּדוּנִי, בַּתַּפּוּחִים: כִּי־חוֹלַת אַהֲבָה, אָנִי.

יוֹנָתִי בְּחַגְוֵי הַסֶּלַע, בְּסֵתֶר הַמַּדְרֵגָה, הַרְאִינִי אֶת־מַרְאַיִךְ, הַשְׁמִיעִנִי אֶת־קוֹלֵךְ: כִּי־קוֹלֵךְ עָרֵב, וּמַרְאֵיךְ נָאוֶה.

דּוֹדִי לִי וַאֲנִי לוֹ, הָרֹעֶה בַּשּׁוֹשַׁנִּים.

שִׂימֵנִי כַחוֹתָם עַל־לִבֶּךָ, כַּחוֹתָם עַל־זְרוֹעֶךָ.

בְּרַח דּוֹדִי, וּדְמֵה־לְךָ לִצְבִי אוֹ לְעֹפֶר הָאַיָּלִים עַל, הָרֵי בְשָׂמִים.

END NOTES

1.   This is how Patsy Dunn Shanberg taught her daughter Debbi Dunn Solomon to make individual seder plates when she was growing up. Debbi continues this tradition.

2.   Rabbi Shalom Meir Wallach, The Pesach Haggadah, culled from the classic Baalei Musar. Mesorah Publications, LTD. Brooklyn: 1992, p.13.

3.   Rabbi Eliyahu Touger, The Chassidic Haggadah Moznaim Publishing Corporation, New York: 1998, p.28

4.   Moshe Shapiro, The Ohr Sameach Haggadah: Rabbi Uziel Milevsky Targum/ Feldheim, New York: 1998, p.28.

5.   Rabbi Eli Manour & Rabbi David Sutton, The Sephardic Heritage Haggadah. Mesorah Publications, LTD. Brooklyn: 2001. p. 26.

6.   Tamara Cohen, Rabbi Sue Levi Elwell, & Ronnie M. Horn, Ma'ayan Haggadah. New York: 2001, p. 47.

7.   Yitz R. C. Stefansky, The Carlebach Haggadah: Seder: Night with Reb Shlomo. Urim Publications, Jerusalem: 2001. p. 54.

8.   Rabbi Marc D. Angel, A Sephardic Passover Haggadah. Ktav, Hoboken: 1998, p. 21.

9.   Brigette Dayan, Shema. June 2004

10. This information was posted on the women's tefillah network listserv (4/10/01) by Rabbi Sue Fendrick with the permission of Susanah Heschel, who created " the orange ritual" as a symbol of inclusion of gays and lesbains in the Jewish community.

11. This activity was suggested by Dan Milstein.

12. I learned this custom from Rabbi Jeffrey Schein.

13. Rabbi David Arnow, Creating Lively Passover Sedarim. Jewish Lights, Woodstock, VT. 2004, p.103.

14. Rabbi David Arnow, Creating Lively Passover Sedarim. p. 43-50.